THE RUDE AWAKENING OF THEODOR MOODY

THE RUDE AWAKENING OF THEODOR MOODY

PER JACOBSEN

HUMBLEBOOKS

THE RUDE AWAKENING OF
THEODOR MOODY

Copyright © 2023
Per Jacobsen & HumbleBooks

1st edition, 2023
Cover Art: Per Jacobsen

ISBN (paperback): 978-87-94319-15-7
ISBN (hardback): 978-87-94319-16-4

All rights reserved.
No part of this publication may be reproduced,
distributed, or transmitted without permission from the author.

This is a work of fiction.
Any resemblance to real people,
living or dead, is purely coincidental.

This book is dedicated to **Kaare B. Dantoft,** *who, aside from being my oldest and best friend, was also the one who, a long time ago, persuaded me to write my first novel.*

A decision that changed my life.

PART I
THEODOR

"Age may wrinkle the face,
but bitterness wrinkles the soul."

THINGS MARTHA USED TO SAY

CHAPTER 1

"Dad, we have to talk about this."

Theodor Moody stares warily at his son. Part of him sees the little blue-eyed boy in coveralls, whom he, a lifetime ago, taught how to carve wood figurines and put worms on fishhooks. Another part of him sees the adult businessman in an overpriced suit, which he, at this moment, has to convince himself not to disown.

"We don't *have to* talk about anything," Theodor grumbles. "I told you I didn't even go to the supermarket yesterday. So how could I be causing a scene over there while I was sitting in the living room at home, watching TV? Explain that to me, Kevin."

Kevin looks around nervously in the entrance hall of the community house as if he is afraid that the other birthday guests in the event room next door will overhear the conversation.

He's worried they'll think he's as nuts as his dad, Theodor thinks. *Afraid that they might also accuse him of a tantrum that never took place.*

"It's just ... there were several witnesses saying it was you. And I talked to the sheriff, who said he had to calm you down and drive you home."

"The sheriff?" Theodor snorts. "Is it Chuck Anderson you're talking about? You went to school with his kids, played at their house several times when you were a kid. Why do you call him *the sheriff* all of a sudden?"

Actually, Theodor does know why. Kevin wants to emphasize the gravity of the situation by stressing Chuck's position as a law enforcer. A lot can be said about Kevin, but when it comes to manipulating others using words, he's always been quite gifted.

"Well, I don't know," Kevin says. "Chuck, then. What we call him hardly matters. The point is that he encouraged me to talk to you about this."

Kevin hesitates and swallows with an audible click. Whether it's the boy in coveralls or the businessman in the suit that sound is coming from, Theodor can't quite discern.

"It's not the first time something like this has happened, Dad," he says. "You know that. There was also the incident down at the library and all that stuff with your neighbor. Kimberly and I didn't say anything, because ... because, well, we figured it had something to do with when Mom she—"

"Think carefully about what you're going to say next," Theodor hisses. But Kevin doesn't. He continues as if the warning has gone right over his head.

"We figured it was your way of coping with it," he says. "Your way of ... reacting when Mom passed away. But it's been almost two years now, Dad, and stuff like the thing in the supermarket yesterday keeps happening. That's why I spoke to the sher... to Chuck about it, and he's given me a brochure for a place that might be interesting to you."

"You do know that Chuck and I are the same age, right?" Theodor asks. "That we grew up together?"

Kevin stares at him for a long moment.

"I ... don't really know where you're going with that," he says. "But yeah, I know now, at least."

"Did you also know that your dear *sheriff* used to date your mother before I married her? And that he's blamed me for snatching her ever since?"

"Oh, come on, Dad!" Kevin groans, clutching his head. "You're not seriously going to accuse him of being behind some crazy conspiracy against you, are you?"

"I'm just saying it's very interesting how he comes flying along with a brochure as soon as there's the slightest sign of trouble."

"The slightest sign of trouble?" Kevin roars. Apparently, he's no longer concerned about the conversation reaching the rest of their family in the event room. "You almost scared the young girl at the register to death, and the woman in line behind you told the owner she won't shop there anymore unless you get a ban. Is that what you call *the slightest sign of trouble*?"

Theodor opens his mouth to answer, but Kevin isn't done yet. Not at all.

"And all because of a misprint in the price of a frozen chicken! Heck, you could have just shown them the receipt calmly instead of throwing food and ranting about capitalism and whatnot, couldn't you?"

"I told you I wasn't out shopping yesterday," Theodor grumbles as he grabs his coat with fingers that quiver—partly due to his arthritis, partly due to his anger—and pulls it down from the coat rack in the entry hall of the community house.

"Where are you going?"

"Outside. Taking a walk."

Kevin stares at him with narrowed eyes for a moment. Then he nods and reaches for his own coat. "I'll go with you."

"The hell you will. You'll go back to the party, apologize for the commotion if necessary, and make sure this hasn't ruined the day for ... um, for ..."

This time it's Theodor's turn to squint his eyes. He knows it's something with an *I* and an *E*, but the other letters seem to have hidden themselves somewhere deep down in the archives of his mind.

"Irene," Kevin sighs. "Her name is Irene. And she's your sister's granddaughter."

Theodor responds to the snappy comment by shutting the door harder than necessary as he walks out into the graveled parking lot belonging to the community house.

Outside it's getting pretty chilly. Half an hour ago, from the window, he watched the sun crawl into hiding behind the horizon line over the fields. Now, a couple of violet clouds in the distance are the only sign that it was there.

He rummages in his pocket for his cigarettes while listening to the voices from inside the event room. Listening for the sound of his own name.

It isn't mentioned—or perhaps his old ears just aren't able to discern that one word from the rest. That's not unlikely either.

It takes all of seven attempts before he manages to get a flame from the lighter, but after pulling the first tar cloud into his lungs, he decides that it was well worth it. God knows, he needs the calming effect of tobacco after that conversation.

The sheriff has given me a brochure. Lord almighty!

Who the hell do they think they are? It's one thing to accuse him of going haywire in the supermarket—which, by the way, is such an incredible story that he can hardly blame Kevin for buying into it. Too amazing to be a fabrication, as they say. Another, far worse, thing is to use such a preposterous story as an excuse to send one's elderly father off to some nursing home.

While Theodor is standing there in the parking lot with his back turned toward his family inside the community house, the autumn wind grows stronger. This causes the arthritis pain to flare up in his fingers, and he has to take turns using his right and left hand to hold the cigarette while the free hand goes into his coat pocket.

During one of these shifts, while pulling his left hand out of his coat pocket, a small, crumpled ball of paper comes out along with it. It falls to the ground and rolls forward a few feet, after which it finds shelter from the wind in a small depression in the gravel.

Theodor stares at it for a long time. Once you've reached his age, it's worth spending some time pondering before deciding to pick up items below knee height. But when the answer doesn't come on its own, and his curiosity only seems to increase, he eventually has to bite the bullet.

Groaning and panting, he bends down and picks up the ball of paper.

You were attended by ... is the first thing that catches Theodor's eye as he unfolds the paper. It's printed in italics at the bottom of the paper, and below it is a name: *Emma.*

You almost scared the young girl at the register to death, Dad!

The next thing that catches Theodor's eye is the third item on the list.

Chicken/Frozen Goods: $5.95.

With an unnerving premonition and a tightening sensation in his stomach, he lets his gaze drift to the upper right corner of the receipt, where the date is printed.

October 9th.

Yesterday, in other words.

He raises a trembling hand to his lips, only to find that the cigarette no longer is between his fingers. It lies in the gravel in front of him, sending a thin snake of grayish-white smoke across his freshly polished dress shoes. He steps on it, twists his foot from side to side, and lifts it again.

The smoke snake gets thinner for a couple of seconds, but then starts growing again. Theodor lifts his foot and stomps it down a few more times, but to no avail. The smoke keeps rising; an ashen ghost hand crawling up his legs, forming a cloud around him and quietly enveloping his world in a haze of gray.

He coughs and gasps for air as he tries to focus on the paper in his hand and decipher the words. They disappear in a mixture of fog and silvery spots swirling randomly around his field of vision.

Call for Kevin, he orders himself. *You're having a heart attack!*

But he can't. When he opens his mouth and tries to shout for help, his throat clenches. Besides, it would hardly be heard, because inside the event room, someone has told a joke that causes a roar of laughter.

You're going to die here, Theodor thinks. *You're going to die in an empty parking lot while your entire family is laughing in the room right next to you.*

This is the last thought going through Theodor Moody's head that night before his legs give way and let him collapse lifelessly on the gravel.

CHAPTER 2

"Oh, you're awake?" a woman's voice whispers from far away. "Let me see if I can find Doctor Mathews. He was the one who operated on you, and he asked me to get ..."

The rest of the words disappear into the same blurred jumble of impressions that have characterized Theodor's universe for the past 24 hours. Down into a dream well filled with flashing lights, oxygen masks, hair nets, concerned voices, curtains, needles, and white coats.

"Oh, so you're awake?" is said once again, but this time the voice belongs to a man, and it cuts clearly through the bubble that Theodor is wrapped in. "I'm glad I got a chance to talk to you before I leave."

Theodor squints, looks down at himself—IV tube in the arm, cannula in his nostrils—and then up at the silhouette in the white coat, which slowly turns into a man who can't be much younger than himself.

"What have you done to me?" he stammers.

Over the collar of the white coat, a wry smile appears on the doctor's lips.

"Nothing but save your life," he says. "You had a cerebral hemorrhage. Fortunately, a very mild one."

A brain hemorrhage. So not a heart attack, which had been his own diagnosis just before he passed out.

"And even though it's a bit of a cliché," the doctor continues, still with a broad smile, "you were quite lucky. If your son hadn't seen you fall over out there, there's no way of knowing what ..."

A brochure for a place that might be interesting to you.

"Is he here?"

"Who? Your son?"

"Yeah, my son, Kevin. Is he here?"

The doctor shakes his head.

"No, he stopped by earlier today, him and his wife. I think they were the ones who brought you the flowers."

Theodor looks over at the bouquet on the bedside table to his right.

Oh yeah, no doubt there. Only his inane daughter-in-law would be insensitive enough to choose a bouquet with the head of a pink orchid as the centerpiece.

And only Kevin could care little enough to miss that detail.

From the flowers, Theodor's gaze slides down to his

own hand, lying limply on his stomach. He raises it and turns it so that the palm of his hand appears.

Of course, the receipt is no longer there, but he can picture it just as clear as day. He remembers it. And he also remembers the incident at the supermarket now. In fact, it feels as though many of the broken connections in his brain have somehow been soldered back together after his awakening, suddenly allowing him to remember a great deal of both good and bad things.

"Are they coming back?"

The doctor shakes his head again.

"Visiting hours are over for today, but they'll probably come by tomorrow, don't you think?"

Theodor responds with an almost inaudible grunt and then starts to pull off his blanket.

"Excuse me, what do you think you're doing?" the doctor asks.

"I'm going to the toilet," Theodor grumbles.

"Sorry, but that's a firm no. Not unless you want to fall over and risk adding a broken hip to your list of ailments."

Theodor bites his front teeth into his lower lip and chews on it, staring angrily at the doctor. Nothing in the world would satisfy him more right now than jumping out of bed and giving that white-coated clown a kick in the ass.

The only problem is that Theodor's body, from the

hip down, agrees with the diagnosis. His legs feel like two sandbags, heavy and motionless.

"It's going to take a while," the doctor says. "But the staff at the rehabilitation center are very good, so if you make sure to follow their instructions, you'll get back on your feet in no time."

He struts, with a hint of a smile on his face, over to the wall behind Theodor's bed, where he pulls a string. Then he walks over to the other side of the bed and takes something out from behind the bedside table where the callous flower arrangement from Theodor's son and daughter-in-law stands.

"Oh, hell no," Theodor grumbles when he sees the wheelchair. "I'm not going to be chugged around in that!"

"You'll have to take that up with the nurse, Mr. Moody," the doctor says. "I just called her. But it's this ... or a bedpan."

Theodor's answer comes in the form of a scoff and a frown. Both are flatly ignored by the doctor, who is more interested in the dial on his wristwatch.

"Unfortunately, I can't stay here any longer," he says, smiling. "But we'll see each other again tomorrow, Mr. Moody. Until then, try to keep your spirits up. Perhaps it'll help when Dina comes in here shortly. That's the name of the nurse on duty tonight, and she's really nice."

My spirits will rise the minute you're out the door, Theodor thinks. But what he says out loud is, "I'll try."

The doctor nods, still with that annoying smile on, and then he turns around and walks toward the door.

When he's gone, Theodor keeps staring at the closed door for a while, almost as if he wants to make sure it wasn't just a joke and that the doctor won't come leaping in through it again.

The doctor doesn't, and Theodor's gaze slowly slides away from the door and to the right.

Not that it's much of an improvement. Because in this direction, his field of vision is filled by the flowers. By the flamboyant bouquet that his daughter-in-law probably put there—without even considering that the pink orchid in the middle is a metaphorical shovelful of salt in Theodor's open wound.

A lily, a dyed rose ... heck, even an orchid of any other color would have been tolerable.

But choosing Martha's favorite flower. Of all the flora of this world ... Christ!

Maybe it wasn't even a slipup? Maybe she was being deliberately mean?

Stupidity or malice? Frankly, neither would come as a surprise to him.

If he could reach it without having to get out of bed, he would take that damned flower, open the window, and throw it—

His stream of thought fades and disappears like the sound of a radio being turned off.

The flower, it's ... moving?

Not the bouquet, not the other flowers. The pink orchid—the flower that, in the 48 years he got with his wife, had always been her favorite. It, and it alone, is moving.

Unable to do anything but gawk, Theodor stares at the orchid. As if pushed by invisible hands, it tilts from side to side a few times. Next, it begins to bend forward over the edge of the vase. Its green stem bends, twists and turns, bends, bends, bends, bends and ...

A sound, a faint *'pop'*, like when you burst a bubble in a piece of bubble wrap, and then the top half of the flower falls onto the table, while the rest of the torn stem stays in the vase.

It must be his imagination. It must have already been on the verge of breaking, and then it just happened at the most improbable moment. Or he must have fallen asleep at some point after the conversation with the doctor, and then his subconscious—

"Mr. Moody?" says a woman's voice behind him. "You pulled the string?"

Theodor turns his head and sees a nurse standing in the doorway.

"I, um ... something happened to the flower," he stutters. "It broke. By itself."

Hearing himself say it out loud, he realizes how crazy it sounds ... how crazy it makes *him* sound. So, when the nurse squints and tilts her head, he clears his throat and says:

"It was the doctor who pulled the string. I need to go to the toilet, and he says I can't do it myself. That I'm to be transported in *that* thing."

The nurse continues to stare at him with narrowed eyes. Then her gaze shifts to the wheelchair that he is pointing to, and she smiles.

"Oh my. Well then, let's see if we can get you to the restroom, Mr. Moody. Let me just get you free of the tubes."

CHAPTER 3

The doctor was wrong. Kevin and Kimberly didn't come back the next day—nor the one after that. In fact, two full days go by before they show up.

However, it would be a lie if Theodor claimed to be surprised by either of those things. On the one hand, he saw doctors get things wrong so often during Martha's illness that you'd think they had a bet going, and on the other hand, he knows that oh-so-busy Kevin wouldn't dream of tearing two consecutive days out of the calendar to visit his father.

What does surprise Theodor, however—quite a lot, at that—is the degree of his son's cynicism.

Because when Kevin walks through the door of the room that Theodor has been given at the rehabilitation center, he is not alone.

It's bad enough that he's dragged Kimberly along,

although she at least hasn't brought any pink orchids this time, but Kevin has also brought another guest.

Chuck Anderson. The sheriff.

"Hi, Dad."

"What is he doing here?"

Kevin, with a feigned expression of confusion, looks over at Chuck and then back at Theodor.

And then, as is often the case, he lets his wife answer for him.

"You could at least say hello when people say it to you, Theodor," she says, staring at him judgmentally with her small, prickly eyes. "Kevin has been very worried, just so you know."

Theodor grunts out a noise that only a very optimistic person would interpret as a *hello*, and then lets his gaze drift over to Chuck.

"What are you doing here?"

Chuck smooths out a fold between two of the buttons of his uniform and nods.

"Kevin asked me to come along. He ... thought it would be a good idea."

He takes a breath, as if he's about to say something more, but is then immediately interrupted by Kevin.

"How are you, Dad? You look a lot better than the other day."

"Yeah, I'll say," Kimberly promptly interjects, after which they both pull their lips up in the same bogus smiles.

27

Smiles that can only mean one of two things: *By the way, Dad, did you get a chance to look at that stuff about the will?* or *We just saw the most beautiful nursing home. Sweet staff, beautiful surroundings. The whole shebang.*

For a moment, Kevin's hand slides up to the inside pocket of his suit jacket—Theodor has a pretty good idea as to what that pocket contains—but then his son hesitates and moves his hand down on the bed rail instead.

"Are they treating you okay?" he asks.

"Well, they visit me every day," Theodor replies, shrugging his shoulders.

"And what about the food? Are you getting enough to eat?"

Kimberly is the one asking these last two questions, and Theodor has to bite his lower lip so as not to bark at her. That woman has been commenting constantly on his eating habits since Martha passed away. Poked at him because of his weight, told him that good, raw ingredients are much better than the prepackaged meals he typically throws in the microwave. Hidden away his sugar bowl.

Oh well, technically, he doesn't have evidence that she's to blame for the sugar bowl—but he has a strong suspicion.

"I'm eating, yeah," he snaps. "And speaking of it, I actually think dinner time is coming up again soon, so ... maybe you should get to the point?"

For a moment, Kevin acts confused, but then Kimberly puts a hand on his arm.

Kevin sighs, nods, and then brings his hand back up to his jacket. This time it reaches all the way into the inner pocket, where it finds a brochure, which he hands to Theodor.

"I'm not looking to start another fight," he says. "And I know you don't remember what happened down in the supermarket, but actually that's one of the main reasons why we—"

"I remember," Theodor mumbles as he studies the brochure with increasing indignation.

RIDGEVIEW CARE CENTER—A DIGNIFIED & MEANINGFUL LIFE is written on the front page.

Below the text are pictures of four elderly people. Two of them play chess, big smiles. Of the other two, one eats a salad, big smile, while the other pedals away —with a big, fat smile, of course—on an exercise bike.

Three activities of which Theodor doesn't find a single one particularly MEANINGFUL.

"Let me get this straight," Kevin says from behind the top edge of the brochure. "You say you do remember what happened down at FullCart?"

Theodor nods.

"Yeah, it was a very unfortunate misunderstanding."

"A misunderstanding?"

"Uh-huh. And yes, I probably overreacted a bit. Honestly, I don't know why I couldn't remember it before ... but maybe my head was already starting to act up when the two of us talked. Because of the stroke, you know."

Kevin stares at him with the expression you'd expect to find in a chess player trying to figure out his opponent's strategy.

"Um, yeah," he says. "But it's not the first time something like this has happened, Dad. There have been other times where you've ... forgotten some pretty unfortunate situations."

"The kids you scolded down by the sports field, for example," Chuck says. "You denied that afterward too. Stubbornly."

It is a well-chosen card that the sheriff throws on the table—and he knows it. The faint smile under his light brown mustache reveals that much.

Because yes, that episode is also among the many that have miraculously been moved back into place in Theodor's memory archives after the stroke ... but it's not one he's too proud of.

"Were they the ones with the kite?" Kimberly asks in her aggravating, nasal voice, and when the sheriff responds with a nod, she rolls her eyes and lets out a resigned sigh.

"There were cars," Theodor explains. "How dumb do you have to be to fly a kite right next to a parking lot full of cars?"

"No one said it was a good idea," Chuck says. "And

had you just explained to them why it was a bad idea and asked them nicely to stop, I probably wouldn't have gotten a call from little Stephen Patterson's parents that night."

"I *told* them to stop," Theodor tries to interject, but Chuck simply raises his voice.

"He wet his pants, Theodor. You scolded those three boys so badly that Patterson's kid peed his pants in fear."

The words are left hanging in the air as his three guests stare at him, awaiting his response.

The problem is that Theodor can't conjure up more than a raspy hum that verges on being a growl.

And as if their three sets of indignant eyes aren't enough, a fourth one has now joined in. They belong to the cleaning lady—a small, skinny woman, Chinese or whatever she is—who has stopped in the hallway, just outside the open door. She also gawks at him as if he were some new animal species.

"We've put it off for far too long, Dad," Kevin says. "But it can't go on. You have to get some kind of help. That's why we, um ..."

He points with a slightly quivering finger to the brochure lying on the blanket beneath Theodor's hands.

"It's a fine place, Theodor," Chuck takes over. "Beautiful surroundings, skilled staff. I can vouch for it. And I know the place because it's where we, um ... it's where my mother moved to when she couldn't manage the farm anymore."

31

"Only a week ago I changed a couple of roof tiles on the garage," Theodor grumbles, ignoring the sheriff and meeting his son's gaze instead.

"Um ... okay?" Kevin says. "I'm not sure what that has to do with this?"

Of course, you aren't. You've probably never changed a single roof tile in your life out of fear of staining your suit, Theodor thinks. What he says out loud, though, is:

"My point is that I'm not some frail old lady and I don't live on a farm. I live in a house which I've maintained for almost forty years—and which I can easily maintain for ten more!"

"But you don't just have the house to think about, Theodor," Kimberly interjects. "What about the cabin up in Maiden Lake? Do you also maintain that? Have you even been up there since Martha passed away?"

"So, we finally got to the heart of the matter, huh? Funny, how the two of you always find a way to turn the conversation over to that cabin."

"Dad, listen, you—"

"No, Kevin. Now *you* listen! Listen carefully! Your mother is gone, but the house on Rue Lane is still my home, and it will stay that way. I'll have to be carried out when I leave my house. And as long as it's my name written on the deed, the cabin in Maiden Lake is also still mine. Whether I use it or not doesn't concern you at all!"

The room in which he has been lodged isn't terribly

large; eighty, maybe ninety square feet. Nevertheless, Theodor could have sworn that the echoes of the last two words can be heard as clearly as if they had been in a cathedral.

In the silence that follows, he must withstand the weight of not only Kevin's but also Kimberly's and the sheriff's stares. Their accusatory, condescending, disgruntled, and—worst of all—worried stares. As if they genuinely feel sorry for him and are just waiting for him to realize that they obviously know what's best for him.

But Theodor is not going to give them that win. He's not even going to leave room for doubt. Therefore, he stubbornly keeps his eyes open and icy as he looks back and forth between them. And as in the schoolyard games of his childhood, he does it without blinking—for so long that it feels like someone has started polishing the outer edges of his eyeballs with sandpaper.

"Okay," Kevin finally says. "I see that you're not crazy about the idea of the care center. But something needs to be done. If there are more episodes like what happened at FullCart, then we may be forced to, um ..."

"What Kevin is trying to say is that it can't go on like this," Kimberly interjects. "And if it does, then your family may have to make the decision *for* you instead of *with* you."

A deluge of resentment washes over Theodor, and

33

he has to fight to keep his anger from taking over. Still, part of him would like to rip the cord out of the big, clunky heart rate monitor they've hooked him up to and strangle her with it.

Of course, he'd never do that. Besides, that would be the equivalent of throwing a bunch of large logs on their bonfire right now.

But Christ. Forcibly enrolling him? Is there no limit to their madness?

"How about a helper then?" Kevin cautiously asks. "Someone who could come to your house and lend a hand with all the practical stuff."

"The practical stuff?"

"Yeah, cleaning, cooking, shopping. Those kinds of things."

"Someone who could run errands for me so I can stay home. Something like that?"

"Well, yeah, for instance."

"Making it so I don't have to go to the supermarket anymore?"

It takes a moment for Kevin to realize that his strategy has been compromised—and before his son has a chance to save the sinking ship, Theodor raises his hand and points at the door.

"Out."

"Dad, just wait."

"Thank you for your visit, but I'm tired now and I need to rest."

"Theodor, you can't just—" Kimberly starts. But Theodor can, and he does.

"GET OUT!"

For a moment, all three of them gape at him in pure astonishment. Then they slowly turn around and walk toward the doorway.

However, before they leave, Kevin seizes the chance to get the last word.

"Think about it, Dad. And take it easy for a while, okay?"

CHAPTER 4

And take it easy for a while, okay?

If one didn't know any better, it might sound as if Kevin was actually worried about his father.

But Theodor does know better. He knows Kevin's little word games, and he understands what those words really were.

A threat. *One more incident like the one down in the supermarket, and then old pop's voice won't be heard at all the next time there's talk of nursing homes.*

A movement, something out in the hallway, catches Theodor's eye and he turns his head. All he has time to detect is a light blue silhouette that's disappeared behind the door frame before he can focus properly.

The cleaning lady?

He lets his gaze drift down to the floor of the hallway. Yup, it looks wet. It must be her.

For God's sake, does she really need to use that much water?

From the floor, his gaze slides over to the brochure, which is no longer lying on his blanket but is on a small table next to the bed.

It's slightly crumpled ... but at least he refrained from ripping it in half.

Like the pink orchid.

That thought turns his eyes to the right and slightly up, where they meet the bouquet. Some gentle soul among the rehabilitation center's staff has made sure it came along when he was moved over here.

The broken stem is still there, and for some reason, the sight of it causes Theodor's blood pressure to rise.

Take it easy for a while, okay?

But how is he supposed to do that when they pull a stunt like that, teaming up with the sheriff, and cornering him like some wounded animal?

All on top of having to sit here, tied to a heart rate monitor, with legs that refuse to do his bidding. He's unable to do anything but stare at the broken stem of that stupid—

He gets no further before he stiffens and hears himself let out a half-choked, gurgling gasp.

What he had dismissed as a crazy coincidence is happening again. This time, though, it's not just a single flower moving on its own. It's the entire bunch ... and the vase.

Unable to comprehend what is happening, he stares at the flowers, which are now starting to slide apart and move out of the vase, floating freely in the air. It's like watching a transmission from a space station, where things float loosely between the astronauts.

Under the vase, the bedside table also begins to move, first in small jerks, then in a slow arc, as it abandons contact with the floor and floats upward.

Theodor closes his eyes and opens them again. One, two, three times he does it ... and the scenario stays the same.

The flowers swirl around each other in the air like dancers at a ball, while the vase and bedside table slowly catch up with them.

A hard pull on his left forearm causes him to twitch and turn his head.

The heart rate monitor is the culprit. Lifted by the same invisible force as the other things, it now hangs at an angle up in the air—so far away from him that the cord has been stretched out and therefore pulls at the bracelet around his wrist.

It's uncomfortable, but Theodor doesn't even have the sense to take off the bracelet and make it stop. Because now, his eyes have found something else.

There are several things to choose from, as the cupboard next to the sink was left ajar, which means that various rags, alcohol bottles, and medical equipment are now floating around.

Yet, it's the glass Theodor can't force his eyes away from. The half-full glass of water that stood on the sink but now floats—upside down—without as much as a drop of water falling out.

He opens his mouth and tries to call for help, but the shock and fear have placed an invisible noose around his neck and tightened it.

Without thinking, he grabs the top edge of his blanket, pulls it to the side, and tries to swing his legs over the edge of the bed ... but, of course, they still aren't listening to him. Not even when he hammers a clenched fist into his thighs, trying to wake them up.

A loud gasp from the door makes him look up—and at the very same moment, the invisible force making things float suddenly disappears.

Gravity is back and everything comes crashing down. Glass and porcelain shatter and water splashes out on the floor as both of them stare at the phenomenon with wide-open, terrified eyes; Theodor from his place in the bed, and the tiny Asian woman in the blue uniform from her spot over in the doorway.

The cleaning lady.

When it's over, he meets her gaze. Dark brown eyes, full of confusion and uncertainty.

And then, his son's voice returns like a distant echo in the back of his mind.

Think about it, Dad. And take it easy for a while, okay?

PART II
YUKI

"My hair is not gray.
It's silver, you old fart."

THINGS MARTHA USED TO SAY

CHAPTER 5

Like many women in similar relationships, Yuki Rowley lives by two sets of rules: the official set, which means the things he outright forbids her to do, and the unofficial set, which consists of things she tries to avoid doing because she knows they make him angry.

And he's not nice when he's angry.

The official rules are fairly easy. In fact, most of them can be described by the word *keep*.

Keep the house, *keep* the garden, *keep* the food warm, *keep* tears and opinions to yourself, and *keep* quiet when he's reading the newspaper, watching TV, thinking, and/or talking. The latter including both phone calls and conversations with others face to face. Especially colleagues from work.

The unofficial rules are more tricky as they can vary depending on his mood. An example could be her use of makeup. On some days, he'll complain that she never tarts up. That she looks like a boring housewife that no one wants to ruffle up.

That's what he calls it; *ruffle up.*

On other days, her wearing makeup can send him all the way up in the red zone. Then she's a cheap tramp who does nothing but strut around, leading other men on.

Both—her with and without lipstick—can make him angry. *Extremely* angry.

For the same reason, she thought it through very carefully this morning before pulling on the red dress and applying the makeup that she is now freshening up in front of the mirror in the theater's restroom.

Today, she hit the mark. Dean didn't get angry when he came home from work and saw that she had jazzed up. He seemed pleased.

This thought was confirmed when they got into the car after dropping Sammy off at Dean's parents' house. Before starting the car, he put his hand on her thigh and whispered that it was almost a pity they were planning to go to the theater. That he could easily think of something better to do.

Her answer? A frozen smile. The exact same one that her twin behind the mirror's glass puts on now as she prepares to go back out to her husband.

She's gotten pretty good at strapping that smile on

by now, although, if you look closely, you can tell that the eyes aren't following suit.

With that thought, Yuki turns her back on herself and walks out of the restroom.

Dean is standing at the bar, one hand resting on the edge of the counter and the other closed around a whiskey glass as if he were the lead actor in a James Bond movie.

He's a good-looking man. You can't take that away from him, despite everything. All the usual boxes are ticked off; tall, charismatic, and in excellent shape.

And should there be any doubt, all it takes is one look at the female theater guests passing by Dean at the bar. Almost without exception, they all steal an extra glance in his direction before they get too far away.

Yuki, of course, understands them well. The same things also blinded her when she first met Dean.

Heck, for her, it was even worse. When he came into her life, he wasn't just a good-looking guy at a bar. He was her savior. A true American hero, police uniform and everything, who ripped open a container door and —in blinding backlight—stepped in to save her and eight other Thai women from a life in chains.

That's what she thought at the time, anyway. Now she knows that it was just an alternative life in chains he offered her.

So, for Yuki's sake, the women at the theater bar are most welcome to take him. And keep him.

47

"You took your sweet time," Dean grumbles as she approaches him. "You're lucky the bar was open. Otherwise, I might not have stayed."

She smiles her frozen smile and settles for thinking her answer.

"Hell," he laughs, throwing the last bit of whiskey down his throat. "I probably wouldn't even have stuck around until the end of that crap show if the bar wasn't open."

Yuki says nothing. She rarely does if it's not necessary.

That the play was not to his liking is no big surprise, though. Dean Rowley prefers entertainment that includes at least one car chase and a few explosions.

Neither was present in the theatrical production of the film classic As *Good as it Gets* that they just saw. Dean did, however, seem to find it quite amusing when Melvin Udall's gay neighbor was beaten to a pulp on stage.

That wasn't a surprise either. The rainbow-colored flag has about the same effect on Dean as a piece of red cloth has on a bull.

"You ready?" he asks as he puts his empty glass on the bar counter.

Yuki opens her mouth to say yes, but then realizes it's not true.

She's *not* ready. She is missing something.

You put it on the backrest of your seat when you sat

down inside the theater, she thinks, feeling a rush of panic. *If you're lucky, it might still ...*

She doesn't get any further before her eyes catch the unmistakable pattern—bronze leaves on dark blue fabric—that characterizes her scarf.

Her scarf, which now hangs on the arm of a young man as he walks around among the theater guests, undoubtedly looking for its owner.

There goes your favorite scarf. That's what you get for not being more careful. You're such a klutz.

She jolts as Dean grabs her elbow and squeezes it.

"I asked if you were ready," he says. Not angrily, but with obvious irritation in his voice.

"What? Yeah, sorry."

Dean doesn't answer, he just drags her with him toward the exit. She follows along, making sure to keep up ... because now, she's said her goodbyes and accepted the loss. Besides, it's just a piece of cloth, nothing to cry about. And certainly not worth taking a—

"Excuse me, ma'am?"

She stiffens and holds her breath, hoping she's not the one being spoken to.

"Excuse me," the young man behind her repeats. "But I think you left your scarf in the theater hall."

She turns around slowly until she is face to face with the kind soul who, in all probability, has just turned the rest of her evening into a living nightmare.

"I was afraid you'd already left, but then I saw you," he says as he holds out the scarf. "This is yours, isn't it?"

"Y-yeah. It's mine."

She accepts the scarf, making sure not to touch the young man's hand in the process. Because she can feel the weight of Dean's gaze on her own hand.

Once she's got the scarf in her hands, she doesn't know what to do for a moment, and she ends up staring awkwardly down at it.

"You're not gonna say thank you, Yuki?" Dean asks. "This poor young man has been scurrying around all over, looking for you."

"Yes, um ... yes, of course. Thank you very much."

"Oh, that's all right," the young man says, pulling his lips up in a wide smile.

His teeth are pearly white. So are the knuckles of Dean's clenched hand, Yuki notices out of the corner of her eye.

For a terrible moment, she's afraid the two will meet—the young man's teeth and Dean's fist—but it doesn't happen. Instead of sending his hand straight forward, Dean slides it under her arm.

"Well, we'd better get going," he whispers through clenched teeth. "We have to pick up Sammy."

Without waiting for an answer, he drags her with him—not so violently that it's suspicious but hard enough to make her upper arm hurt a bit. Simultaneously, he forms a gun with the thumb and forefinger of his free hand, points it at the young man, and winks at him as if to say: *You're the man, kid!*

By the time they've left the foyer and entered the theater's semi-dark parking lot, the finger gun has been packed away again. However, Dean's other hand isn't going anywhere. It maintains its grip on her arm as they walk to the truck.

The autumn wind is cold, but it's nothing compared to the chills Yuki feels once she's taken a seat in the vehicle.

It's the sound that triggers them. The sound of the locks automatically clicking when she and Dean close the doors. Her nerves blow it completely out of proportion, making it resound in her head as if it were the sound of locking bolts in a bank vault. Or a prison cell.

Dean puts the key in the ignition but doesn't turn it right away. He just sits and stares blankly out the windshield.

A few yards farther ahead is a streetlamp, but the truck's roof eats up most of its light, so only the bottom of his face can be seen. Still, it's enough. Everything she needs to know is revealed by the way he's chewing on his lower lip.

He has the same unconscious habit when playing poker with his work buddies and he has been given either a very good or a very bad hand. In other words, this is what he looks like when he's planning.

And the only thing worse than a spontaneous outburst of anger from Dean Rowley is one he's had time to think about and design.

She twitches as he suddenly raises his hand ... but it doesn't touch her. It grabs the key and turns it.

The pickup growls to life, and Dean starts backing out, pretending he didn't even notice her jerking uneasily in her seat.

But he did. And he found it amusing. Although his face is now completely out of the light of the streetlamp, she can still make out his smile in the dark.

In tense silence, she sits in the seat, fiddling with the hem of her dress, awaiting the inevitable.

She knows it's coming. The only question is *when* he's gonna let go of the steering wheel and reach for her.

Outside, the night glides by; its blurred lights drawing multicolored lines across a black canvas.

Inside the vehicle, there is no display of colors. Everything appears despairingly black and gray. To some extent, though, Yuki's other senses make up for the lack of visual impressions. Her ears register every little sound, and her nose clearly picks up the faint undertone of whiskey drifting in the air every time Dean exhales.

After the first couple of miles, she starts to consider that she might have been wrong ... and after two more, she starts to *believe* it. Especially since they have now entered Gleamsdale, which is the town where Dean's parents live—and where they have to pick up Sammy.

And Dean usually doesn't do anything to her in front of Sammy. She wishes she could say it was for the sake of the boy, but the more likely explanation is that a testimony from Sammy would complicate things unnecessarily.

The same is also the reason why it's only when Dean loses his temper completely that a punch will land outside of the zones on her body which can be covered with clothing. He is a cop, after all. He knows *how* and *where* to land a punch to avoid raising any alarms.

But now they've actually entered the street where his parents live, so maybe there will be no need to cover anything at all this—

That's how far she gets before the house slides by, and she realizes what it was that went through his head when he was biting his lower lip earlier. What he was planning.

"You ... drove past their house?" she stammers. "Did you forget that we have to pick up Sammy?"

He glances at her and makes a faint, snorting sound.

"I can do that later," he says. "My folks can easily keep him another hour or two. And right now, I think we just need to get home, don't you?"

Yuki tries to force out a smile, but this time she comes up short. Because there was one word—undoubtedly a carefully chosen one—in the sentence Dean said that has her paralyzed.

I. Not *we*. He said that *he* could pick up Sammy later. Not that *they* could do it.

"I don't know about that, Dean," she says uneasily. "Sammy's got school tomorrow, and—"

"Oh, come on," he interrupts, sending her a smile that makes her think of the Cheshire cat from *Alice in Wonderland*. "You don't expect me to believe that you squeezed into that dress just because we were going to the theater, do you?"

For a moment, she doesn't even understand what he's raving about. Then the realization hits, and she catches herself pulling down on the dress, trying to cover her knees.

"But then again, maybe it wasn't your husband's attention you were hoping to catch with that little red thing."

"I don't know what you're talking about."

"Maybe it was the young punk who brought you the scarf that you'd ... forgotten?"

"Dean, listen ..."

"Was that why you spent so much time in the restroom? Because you were hoping he'd follow you in there with the scarf, so he could *give it to you*? Maybe you were hoping for a—"

"Dean, please. Listen to me. It's not like that. I forgot my scarf by mistake, and he just gave it back to me. That's all."

She has barely finished the sentence before she realizes her crime—and gasps.

She has broken a rule, and it is not even one from the unofficial set. It's one of the main rules, one of the big ones from the *Keep* list.

Keep your mouth shut when he speaks.

The pain is immediate and intense as his hand shoots toward her, grabbing the skin of her stomach. The fingers dig in, below the ribs, and squeeze, making it feel like the bones are shattering.

"Why do you insist on doing shit like this?" he snarls. "Why do you always have to push me to the point where I have to punish you?"

As he speaks, he twists his hand around, giving her the sensation that all the muscles in her diaphragm are being ripped apart.

Without her being able to do anything to prevent it, an acidic fluid foams up through her throat, filling her mouth with the taste of vomit. Her stomach screams at her to spit it out, but she forces herself to swallow. Because nothing in the world could save her if she were to throw up in Dean's truck right now.

"You know I hate it when I have to punish you, Yuki. So why do you do it, huh?"

That's a lie. Nothing else can make Dean's eyes glow with excitement in the way that a conviction and its subsequent punishment does.

"I'm ... sorry," she groans. Those two words are all she's capable of squeezing out.

Still with his fingers buried beneath her ribs, Dean stares at her, shaking his head slowly.

"It's not fair," he whispers. "All the shit that I do for you, and then ... hey, what the fuck is going on over there?"

His stern face, which a few seconds ago lay in darkness, is now lit up in flickering blues and reds. For a moment, Yuki thinks it's because she's about to pass out. It's only when Dean lets go of her—letting her gasp in a mouthful of air for her brain—that the context becomes clear:

The flashing lights are coming from outside, specifically from the parking lot in front of the community house in Gleamsdale, where an ambulance is parked alongside a police car.

The latter is probably the reason why her husband instinctively let go of her. After all, the police car could belong to one of Dean's colleagues from the force.

The flickering lights make it difficult to see clearly, but she does manage to distinguish two paramedics carrying a stretcher into the ambulance. On it lies an elderly man.

She opens her mouth to pass on this observation, but even though he himself asked just a moment ago, Dean doesn't seem to care anymore.

His wife, on the other hand, he hasn't forgotten about.

"Don't get too comfortable," he says, rubbing his hand over the top of the steering wheel so it creates a faint, scraping sound. "We're not done talking about this."

He didn't have to point that out. Yuki knows perfectly well that it isn't over.

This was just foreplay. He hasn't even started ruffling her up yet.

CHAPTER 6

An hour, maybe an hour and a half later, Yuki is kneeling in the bathroom in her home, halfway hanging over the edge of the bathtub.

The floor tiles are freezing, and it hurts to be in such an awkward position ... but the bathtub is preferable to spitting blood out on the floor. The red color is virtually impossible to get out of the joints between the floor tiles. Experience has taught her that.

Dean is gone. Once he was done instructing his spouse on right and wrong, there was no need to stick around, so he pulled on a clean shirt and popped over to pick up Sammy from his parents.

How long ago now? Ten minutes? Fifteen? Either way, she'd better get up soon and clean up this mess.

And herself.

With a hand that feels like it's been embedded in a glove made of lead, she reaches out and takes the shower head off its holder. Thankfully, it's hanging on the hook down by the faucet because she used it to wash some mud off Sammy's shoes earlier. Had it been hanging up on the wall holder, it would have taken all her strength just to get it down.

She turns on the hot water and directs the jets at the red stains at the bottom of the tub. The blood and water mix, forming a little, pink river that gradually narrows and eventually disappears down the drain.

All that remains now is the heavy stench of rust hanging in the water vapor ... but she probably won't be able to judge when that's gone, because the same taste predominates in her throat and mouth.

Eight months, she thinks as she turns off the water and lets the shower head drop into the bathtub. *Eight more months, and then it's over.*

That's her own secret *Keep* rule: *Keep yourself alive for another eight months and it's over.*

An idea—a thought that she knows is absurd but still can't push away—burrows down into her, fills her with panic.

What if he's found it?

She twists her torso so she can get her hands on the floor. Then she starts crawling on all fours.

You're too slow! she scolds herself in her mind as she, moaning and panting, reaches the door and pushes it open with her shoulder. *You need to get on your feet. Otherwise, you'll never make it.*

It's not an unreasonable assessment. The bathroom is on the first floor and her destination is the laundry room in the basement. To get there, she has to fight her way down not one, but two flights of stairs—and right now, just getting from her place on the floor all the way over to the stairs seems like an insurmountable task.

The hallway—the floor of which she is currently curled up on—is really nothing more than a kind of ledge. One side is open to the ground floor, except for a wooden railing, which becomes the railing of the stairs farther on.

It takes two attempts before she manages to pull herself up far enough to grab the handrail, and when she finally gets on her feet, the pain is so overwhelming that she's on the verge of spitting out a fresh mouthful of blood—over the edge of the ledge.

Hitting the living room's wooden floor ... or maybe even some of the furniture. Now *that* would have been a death sentence.

Given the circumstances, she's doing okay. Her legs shiver beneath her, and sporadic silver spots appear in her field of vision every time she takes a deep breath, but she *is* moving forward.

You don't need to check it right now. If he has found it, it makes no difference anyway.

True. But the idea is planted in her mind, and she needs to have it either confirmed or denied.

As she rounds the corner of the railing and starts the descent, Yuki decides to sit down and slide down the stairs on her butt.

She uses the same strategy for the basement stairs, even though she perhaps could have handled it walking upright. Her reasoning is simple: Should she fall, she strongly doubts that she would be able to get back up.

The basement consists of two rooms; Dean's workshop and the laundry room, which the stairs—*thank God*—lead directly into.

At the back wall of the laundry room is an old washing machine, and not before she's gotten all the way over to it does Yuki pause to catch her breath. Because it's there, hidden beneath this worn-out, cream-colored machine, her secret lies.

Like a hot iron against her bare belly. That's what it feels like in her diaphragm as she grabs two of the top corners of the machine and pulls.

"Oh, come on, you big blockhead," she moans as she tugs and pulls to get the machine out from the wall. "Help me out, would you?"

After some reflection, the washing machine decides to accommodate her wish. It slides forward. Not much, but enough for her to grab the edge of the loose floor tile behind it.

A new wave of anxiety washes through her as she

lifts it up—and as the answer comes, the relief is so intense that it has her sobbing loudly.

The blue Ziplock bag is still there, and so are its contents. Her salvation, in the form of a matchbox—the old-fashioned, medium-sized kind—with the word *HOTHEADS* printed on it.

Carefully, she takes out the box and caresses its surface as if it were an infant. Then she opens it and lets her gaze drift down over the three rolls of dollar bills packed tightly within.

Eight months. When Sammy turns ten. That's the deadline she set for herself when she made the decision on his birthday just under a year and a half ago. And if she just makes sure to put aside the same amount each month as she has so far, it should be enough for them to survive until she's found a new job and they've settled into the new place. Wherever in the world it may be.

A sound—the heavy, metallic rumble of a grandfather clock's bell—reverberates up in the living room, making her twitch with dread. She quickly packs the box away and puts the tile back in place. Then she grabs the corners of the washing machine again and starts pushing it.

This time, it's easier. It's as if touching the box has somehow strengthened her and enabled her to better endure the pain.

After hiding away her deepest—and most dangerous —secret, Yuki leaves the laundry room. She takes the basement stairs—this time walking upright—and reaches the top step in the exact same second as she hears the front door open.

Footsteps, light and quick. Sammy.

She glances down at herself, scans her lower legs, thighs, arms, shoulders, checking that all the bruises are covered in fabric. Then she pulls it on. The smile. Just in time to let it accompany the words as she steps out in front of the boy and says:

"Hey, sweetie. I've missed you! Did you have fun at Grandma and Grandpa's?"

CHAPTER 7

"Are you okay, Mom?"

"I'm okay, Sammy. Just need to catch my breath."

That's a lie. Yuki is *not* okay. Dean didn't hold back last night, and he has left her with a stomach that feels as if all the tendons are stretched to their bursting point. So, the bike ride, first to Sammy's school and then to her work at the rehabilitation center, is challenging today. On the edge of what she can handle.

"It's just that you're so lightning fast," she says, hoping a bit of small talk will buy her some extra time. "I almost can't keep up."

She lifts her head from the handlebars on which it rested, smiles at him ... and feels her heart sink.

Her smile is not returned. In fact, under his helmet, Sammy's small, freckled face is pulled together in a severe grimace that makes him look years older.

And a bit like his father.

"Are you sick?" he asks.

Yuki opens her mouth to say no, but then she realizes that the boy has just given her the perfect escape route.

"You know what? I think I might be. My head has felt a bit heavy in the past few days. So maybe you're right. Maybe I am getting sick."

He stares at her. *Analyzes* her with his dark brown eyes. Then he nods.

"I'll go slower on the last stretch," he says. "Then you'll be fine."

For a moment, the boy's goodness—and the stark contrast it is to his father's nature—nearly makes Yuki break down in tears, but she bites it down, instead focusing on getting back on the bike.

"Thank you, Sammy," she says as they roll out of the side of the road and start riding the last few hundred yards to the school. "It's nice of you, but I'll try to keep up."

And Yuki does. She pedals as hard as her bruised belly allows, and shortly after, they slow down and stop next to the school's bike racks—where she feels another strike of pain in her diaphragm. One that isn't caused by her husband's fists.

The pain is triggered by two things. The first is the sight of Sammy's smile fading in a split second as if someone has pressed an *Off* button in his brain. The other is the sight of Alex Skinner, a skateboard-rolling, gum-chewing little smartass bastard who is several years older than Sammy, and who in this school year has chosen him to be the victim for every nasty joke that enters his twisted little mind.

"Is he still causing you trouble?"

Sammy shrugs.

"It's not that bad anymore."

"So, it helped when I had that talk with Miranda?"

Sammy nods, and Yuki doesn't feel convinced.

"You'll let me know if anything happens. You have to promise me, okay?"

Sammy nods again. Then he pulls up his bag and starts walking toward the school.

"You better get going, Mom. You're gonna be late for work again."

He is right, of course. By now, McKinney from the rehabilitation center has given her the final warning for being late so many times that she'll have to act on it someday. So yeah, Yuki really has to get going. But not before she's said goodbye.

"See you this afternoon, sweetie. I love you."

The boy responds with a smile and a wave, then disappears through the gate into the schoolyard.

As soon as he is out of sight, Yuki gets back on her bike and drives on. Passing the school, she gets another glimpse of Alex Skinner—now in the company of two other skateboard punks.

That damned little terrorist. Maybe I should ask Dean to have a stern talk with him.

Like a bizarre divine inspiration, shooting down in her without warning, this thought hits Yuki, and she doesn't know whether to laugh or cry.

Because no matter how much she despises the Skinner kid, the image of him at Dean's mercy isn't nice.

CHAPTER 8

Two hours later, Yuki once again finds herself sitting on a cold tile floor with her hand on her stomach.

The floor belongs to the linen room at the rehabilitation center, where she works as a cleaning lady, and the cause of her stomach cramp is the half-full mop bucket in front of her.

There's probably no more than one and a half gallons of water in the bucket. Still, it felt as if one of Dean's punches has been hanging in a time pocket and only hit her stomach a moment ago when she tried to lift it.

Come on, get up! Even McKinney is gonna run out of chances to give you if you show up late all the time and then don't even work while you're here.

Using that thought as motivation, she gets back on her feet and straightens her uniform. Then she grabs the handle and drags the bucket with her, halfway carrying, halfway pulling.

Outside of the linen room runs a long corridor. In the middle of it, her cleaning cart is parked—and right behind that, her boss, Liz McKinney, stands.

McKinney is a robust woman in her fifties, who always wears floral dresses. Maybe it's because she hopes that the very feminine, colorful dresses will compensate for, and move attention away from, her masculine build. Because McKinney doesn't exactly have an hourglass figure. She is built more like an old Volvo—square, sturdy, and reliable.

McKinney's hands, in particular, have always fascinated Yuki. They are huge and rough. The kind you'd expect to find on a dockworker or a farmer.

At this moment, those hands are placed on McKinney's hips. And she doesn't look pleased.

"Yuki ..." she starts, then shakes her head in resignation, as if just saying Yuki's name is tiring her. "Where have you been?"

"Filling this," Yuki replies, nodding down at the mop bucket.

McKinney glances at the bucket, then back at Yuki, but says nothing. Instead, she just waits patiently for the realization to strike on its own.

"You've been standing here a long time?"

McKinney blinks her eyes—*bingo*—and sighs.

"I can explain," Yuki says.

"I know you can. You always can. But this can't go on."

Something in McKinney's voice worries Yuki. At first, she can't put her finger on it, but then it dawns on her; McKinney sounds sad, almost ... despairing? She sounds like an employee of a big corporation who, after countless years of struggle, finally realizes that the promotion will never come.

In the wake of that thought, another follows: This time it's for real. The words that Yuki knows her boss is going to say next aren't empty threats anymore.

"I know I've said it before," McKinney says, "but this *is* the final warning, Yuki. I can't keep turning a blind eye. One more screwup, and then, um ... then you're out of a job. Is that clear?"

Yuki swallows the lump in her throat and nods.

"I'm really sorry, Ms. McKinney. I'll do better, I swear."

"For your own sake, I hope that's true," McKinney says. Then she hesitates and adds, "And for my sake as well. Because I like you, Yuki. You know that. You just need to—"

"I know," Yuki interrupts, her voice on the verge of tears. "And I will."

McKinney hesitates again, this time for a long while.

"Good," she says, placing her dockworker hand on Yuki's shoulder. "Then let's put this behind us and focus on doing better from now on, eh?"

70

Yuki tries to mutter a thank you but manages no more than a faint and rasping vowel sound.

"I'll be in my office if you need anything, okay?"

Following those words, McKinney gives Yuki's shoulder one last squeeze before turning around, walking down the hall, and disappearing through a door at the end.

One more screwup and you're out of a job.

Contrary to what McKinney might think, it's not the threat of the firing per se that had Yuki's voice quivering.

Sure, she likes her job, but it's the other stuff that worries her. The consequences. Having to tell Dean about it. Losing the ability to send money to her family in Thailand as she normally does.

And worst of all, seeing her finish line, eight months in the future, getting pushed forward indefinitely because she no longer has any money to put aside in the matchbox under the washer in the basement.

Discouraged—but also with a stubborn determination born from this imminent threat—Yuki lifts the mop bucket onto the cart. Then she rolls up her sleeves and starts pushing it across the floor of the hallway.

She has work to do now—and she intends on doing it without looking back. With her eyes fixed on the future.

CHAPTER 9

Eager to get her job situation back under control, Yuki has made a plan. She will make sure to be on time every day, she's gonna work her ass off, and she will close herself off to distractions, internal as well as external.

Up until this moment, it has been an excellent strategy, but now, having stopped in the doorway of one of the patient rooms, she is no longer able to ignore the world around her.

There are two reasons for this. Firstly, she is shocked at how the three guests are talking to the old man in room 02—especially considering that one of them is wearing a police uniform—and secondly, she is shocked by the incident that she has just heard one of them describe.

He wet his pants, Theodor. You scolded those three boys so badly that Patterson's kid peed his pants in fear.

That was the phrase that made her stop in the doorway—thus breaking her three-day streak of sticking to the plan.

Three people around an old man in a bed. It's like watching hyenas surrounding a wounded animal, trying to force it into a corner.

This old animal still has some fight left in it, though. Yuki sees that immediately in the old man's eyes as his son says:

"We've put it off for far too long, Dad. But it can't go on. You have to get some kind of help. That's why we, um ..."

Yuki hasn't had the pleasure of speaking with him yet, but the elderly gentleman in the bed has made quite an impression on her coworkers. She has heard them complaining about his negative attitude in the lunchroom on several occasions. And he doesn't exactly sound like a ray of sunshine. Nevertheless, she can't help but feel a pinch of sympathy for him right now. Maybe it's because she's also felt the weight of a *final warning* in the last few days.

"It's a fine place, Theodor," the man in the police uniform says. "Beautiful surroundings, skilled staff. I can vouch for it. And I know the place because it's where we, um ..."

He says something more, but Yuki doesn't catch it, because her ears prioritize the sound of footsteps coming from one of the side aisles. It sounds like they're headed in her direction.

McKinney? Could be.

She grabs the handle of the cleaning cart and rolls it into an empty room two doors ahead. Next, she picks up a cloth and starts wiping down the windowsills and tables while still trying to follow the rest of the conversation in room 02.

She can only pick up fragments, and that's mainly because one of them occasionally raises his voice. Yet, she is able to deduce the main issue: The old man's family wants to have him put in a nursing home. And they threaten to force him, should he give them a reason to.

His answer was clear. Both figuratively and directly.

I'll have to be carried out when I leave my house! were the words that reached her most clearly through the walls. At least until this moment, when his voice reverberates through the corridor behind her.

"GET OUT!"

For a long time, Yuki stands still, halfway bent over the TV she's wiping off, listening for their response to that outburst.

Either it never comes or she's unable to catch it. What she does hear, though, is their footsteps in the hallway as they walk by.

Discreetly, she leans out the doorway and glances

down toward room 02. Then she pulls back again, shaking her head.

Don't. The only thing you need to worry about is washing the hallway floor—and with them gone, now would be a good time. So, get to work!

Determined to follow that order, Yuki readies a bucket and starts mopping the hallway. She does it with systematic, almost mechanical movements, trying to keep her gaze fixed on the floor.

The first time she passes the open door into room 02, she manages not to look inside. The second time, however, her brain senses that something is wrong with what she sees out of the corner of her eye.

Therefore, she lifts her gaze ... and gasps in shock when she sees the old man sitting in the bed.

Surrounded by free-floating furniture and medical equipment.

PART III
SAMMY

"Youth is wasted on the young."

THINGS MARTHA USED TO SAY

CHAPTER 10

Theodor Moody is not a man who's easily browbeaten, and only very few times in his long life has he been in a situation where he has felt genuinely powerless.

This moment, however, is one of those. Not only is he stunned and frightened by the sight of the objects that hovered around him and then crashed to the ground, he is also terribly aware that the cleaning lady in the doorway is holding his fate in her hands.

Think about it, Dad. And take it easy for a while, okay?

Until now, not the slightest peep has come out of her mouth, but should she decide to call a nurse, it's over. The floor is littered with stuff, and the only logical conclusion is that the old, demented lunatic—who, as it happens, was the only person in the room—has gone berserk.

Shazam; a one-way ticket to RIDGEVIEW CARE CENTER.

He wants to tell her it wasn't his fault. That something made the things move on their own. The problem is that he is not able to communicate on any comprehensible level. His throat feels like he's been trying to swallow a tennis ball, and inside his head is a chaotic maelstrom of confused thoughts. He can't even attempt to explain his innocence using gestures because his arms just lie there, like two limp rolls of meat on the blanket.

For a long time, nothing changes. The cleaning lady stares at him, then down at the things on the floor, then back at him. He stares at her, then down at the floor, then back at her.

But then, without warning and without words, she suddenly enters the room, bends down, and begins picking things up. She starts with the contents from the half-open cupboard to the left of the sink. She puts the small alcohol bottles and medical equipment back on the shelves. She does the same with the cleaning cloths from the cupboard. However, she keeps one and uses it to wipe water and shards from the floor where the glass crashed down.

Afterward, she walks around the room, moving the furniture back into place and lifting the heart rate monitor back up. Finally, she picks up the porcelain pieces from the vase and throws them in the trash along with the wrecked bouquet.

She does all of this without saying a word and without even looking at Theodor in the bed.

He, on the other hand, looks at her. With eyes squinted and full of uncertainty, he follows her movements, while trying to figure out her motivation.

It seems like she's trying to help him, but why on earth would she do that? She has nothing to gain by doing that ... does she?

He takes a breath and opens his mouth to ask but is interrupted when another woman—a sturdy woman in a floral dress—pops up in the doorway.

"Is ... um, is everything all right in here?" she asks, glancing at the cleaning lady. "Jameson in 04 called me. He said he heard some ... noise coming from in here."

With a dry throat and his heart racing in his chest, Theodor looks at the cleaning lady, convinced that now is the moment when she'll place the target on his back.

But she doesn't push him into the lion pit. She just shakes her head and smiles at the woman in the doorway.

"It was nothing, Ms. McKinney. A vase that toppled over by accident. That's all."

"A vase?" the woman asks, shifting her gaze to Theodor, who nods and shrugs his shoulders.

For a while, the woman stays in the doorway,

watching him, her arms crossed. Then she finally nods, turns around, and leaves the room.

Straightaway, the cleaning lady follows suit, and before Theodor has a chance to react, he is once more alone in his tiny prison, which consists of a mattress and a bed frame.

The room is dead silent now. Inside his head, however, there is plenty of noise. His thoughts swirl around. Most of them so rapidly that he can't catch a hold of them.

Twice it has happened now. The first time, he wrote it off as being a strange coincidence. He just won't get far with that explanation this time. Because a single, fragile stem breaking while he's staring at it … yeah, well, odd, but not impossible. Several things rising into the air around him without anyone touching them, on the other hand. That's the very definition of impossible.

Hallucinations? A system failure in an aging brain?

Excellent guess … if it wasn't for her. Because how the hell does he explain that the cleaning lady not only witnessed what happened but also cleaned it up afterward?

Unless, of course, she's also just something your old brain made up.

The thought starts as a joke, a kind of ironic comment from Theodor to himself. It doesn't take many seconds, though, before he no longer finds it funny.

Because suddenly it feels like the only plausible explanation.

That it was all just a fabrication.

He has to talk to her. Confirm that she saw the same as him. Confirm that she even exists.

Obsessed with that idea, Theodor stares at the doorway, hoping she'll show up.

She doesn't. To be fair, he does catch a glimpse of her late in the afternoon, but it's not by the door. It's in the street outside the window, where she's standing on the sidewalk with her bike, greeting another cyclist—a young boy.

Her son? Not impossible, but Theodor is not entirely convinced, given that the kid is blond, while she has the same black hair as all the other Chinese people ... or whatever she is.

Either way, the two must know each other well, because when the boy arrives, he gets a big hug from the cleaning lady, after which they get on their bikes and leave together.

The entire scene takes no more than half a minute, but for Theodor, that's beside the point. He saw the cleaning lady.

She was there. She exists.

CHAPTER 11

During the morning hours of the next day, Theodor catches several brief glimpses of the blue lightning bolt whizzing by out in the hallway.

The blue lightning bolt. That's the nickname he's given the cleaning lady because the light blue color of her uniform is usually all he manages to register before she's out of sight again.

At every opportunity, he has tried—unsuccessfully—to get her attention by clearing his throat loudly as she passes the doorway.

Only now, just past noon, has it worked. She has finally stopped—and, of course, this took him by surprise. So now he doesn't know what to say.

"What is it that you want?" she asks softly, almost in a whisper, from the doorway.

She seems cautious and withdrawn, maybe even afraid of him.

Can you blame her? The last time she saw you, half the room was floating in the air around you. Of course, she's scared.

"About what happened yesterday," he stutters, but the rest of the sentence is never completed, as he loses his train of thought, seeing the cleaning lady turn pale and taking a step backward.

For a long time, she remains silent. Then she looks down at her folded hands and asks:

"How'd you do it?"

"I didn't do anything," Theodor replies, shrugging. "It just happened."

The cleaning lady stares at him with watchful, doubting eyes. But at least she stays in the doorway.

"So, um ... it wasn't on purpose?"

"On purpose?" Theodor exclaims. "I'm not even sure that it was me who did it."

That's not entirely true, because even though he didn't have a shred of control, he clearly felt that he was the one who somehow set it in motion. Especially since it all started with the pink orchid.

But as long as it's no more than a feeling, he sees no reason to share it with the cleaning lady. And definitely not now, when the fear on her face gives way to something resembling relief.

"It was scary," she says.

Theodor nods—and decides that her voice sounds restrained enough for him to ask the question that was the real reason for calling her in here.

"Why, um ... why did you help me?"

The cleaning lady pauses for a moment and then nods.

"Where I'm from, we take care of our old."

"Elderly," Theodor grunts because he can't help it, even when he ought to.

"Sorry, what?"

"Elderly," he repeats, holding out an open hand as if he were about to accept some invisible object. "*Old* doesn't sound nice. You should say *elderly* or *elders*."

All at once, the uncertainty and unease seem to have left the cleaning lady, who now crosses her arms and forms a small, thin handlebar with her eyebrows.

"You know, I'm not trying to offend you," Theodor continues. "I know the language can be a challenge for your, um ..."

"For my what?" the cleaning lady asks.

"Yes, well, um, for your ... people."

The cleaning lady stares at him fiercely for a while, before finally giving him a slow nod. But she remains silent.

"Is he your son?" Theodor says, attempting to get the derailed train back on its tracks. "The boy you left with yesterday. Is he your son?"

Still no answer, but her eyes narrow, and the eyebrow handlebars above them move a bit farther down.

"No, not like that," Theodor exclaims when he realizes what it sounds like. "I wasn't watching him. I just happened to see you."

He points toward the window.

"Out there. On the street yesterday."

The cleaning lady takes a deep breath, bites her lower lip, and nods one more time.

"That was my son, yes," she says.

"So, I guess your husband is from here?"

"What do you mean?"

"His hair. Your son is blond, so I take it that your husband is from here."

The cleaning lady tilts her head, adopting a facial expression that Theodor can't decipher. By his analysis, she is just as likely to be on the verge of a nervous breakdown as an outburst of laughter.

"Yes," she says, sighing. "My husband is from the United States. And he's white."

"I thought so."

After those words follows an awkward pause, which none of them manage to break for a long time. Then, suddenly, the cleaning lady turns her gaze down to her wristwatch and says:

"Well, I'd better get back to work. So, um ... if there was nothing else?"

"Oh, yeah, of course," Theodor replies, a bit embarrassed. "Gotta keep the ball rolling."

The cleaning lady looks at him with an expression of mild confusion, which he assumes must be because she hasn't heard that expression before. Then she nods and gives him a frozen smile before disappearing into the hallway.

The rest of that day, he doesn't see the slightest trace of the blue lightning bolt.

CHAPTER 12

"It's for your own good, Mr. Moody," Theodor mutters to his own reflection in the glass wall. "Who the hell does he think he is? That little twat should consider himself lucky I'm still in a wheelchair."

The glass wall belongs to the tiny, outdoor shelter where patients—after the obligatory half-hour lecture on the harmful effects of tobacco from a twenty-something dietician—can be allowed to smoke.

And the words that Theodor repeated to his own mirror image—*it's for your own good, Mr. Moody*—were the closing sentence of that very lecture. There would probably have been more nuggets from the young punk if Theodor hadn't taken matters into his own hands, grabbed the rims of the wheelchair, and rolled out of the room, foaming with anger.

At least the quack hadn't followed him out here.

He was probably terrified that I would blow my poisonous smoke on him, Theodor thinks, chuckling at his own wit.

As he sits there in his glass cage, Theodor sees several people passing by on the street in front of the rehabilitation center. The vast majority slide in and out of his field of vision without him really registering them. They interest him no more than he interests them.

At one point, though, there is one that makes him lower the cigarette from his lips and turn his head.

The boy comes riding down the street, without pedaling, on a blue bike that slowly loses speed and then stops on the opposite side of the road, about thirty yards from Theodor's spot in the shelter.

The cleaning lady's kid. He'd recognize the semi-long, blond hair anywhere. She really ought to get him to a barber! If anyone had shown up with a scruffy mane like that when Theodor went to school, they could look forward to a year in hell.

Except for that, the kid looks pretty respectable. He stays put, waiting for his mother, not even getting out his cell phone. Not many kids would show that kind of patience these days.

Maybe it's because his mother is Chinese? After all, they do have a reputation for setting the bar high for their children. He can probably play the piano too.

Oh, well, maybe Theodor was too quick with his

appraisal after all because now the kid opens his school bag and rummages through it—undoubtedly to get out his phone.

Nope, once again, his theory is put to shame. What the kid pulls out is a comic book that he brings with him over to a bench and starts flipping through once he has taken a seat.

Hm, yeah, a real book would have been better, Theodor thinks. Nevertheless, he has to admit that he is a bit impressed.

A rumbling sound, like that of a small cement mixer, makes him look to the right, where he spots three boys, older than the cleaning lady's kid. They glide across the road at breakneck speed, and it's their skateboards that are producing the sound.

When they are close to the boy on the bench, one of them jumps, thereby moving the skateboard from the road and onto the sidewalk. Then he puts one foot on the ground while the other one kicks forward. As a result, he stays in place while the skateboard continues —straight into the rear wheel of the blond kid's bike, causing it to tip over. Next, he walks over to it and stomps his foot into the same wheel, bending a handful of the spokes.

"What the hell?" Theodor mutters as the skater boy and his buddies burst into laughter at the creative stunt.

On the bench in front of them, the cleaning lady's boy curls up in fear, but he makes no effort to run away

... which tells Theodor one thing with overwhelming certainty: This isn't the boy's first encounter with those thugs.

As a confirmation of that thought, he now hears the skateboard-kicking bully—undoubtedly the leader of the pack—raise his voice and shout:

"Yo, Sammy Salami! What'ya reeading?"

Sammy doesn't answer. He just puts his comic aside on the bench's seat and stares at the ground as if he's hoping they'll disappear if he doesn't look in their direction.

Unfortunately, that strategy works better on the nighttime monsters in the closet of a kid's bedroom than it does on school thugs.

"Yo, Salami, are you deaf? I asked you something! What are you reading?"

While shouting, the chief bully turns to his co-conspirators to make sure that they're witnessing the show. As he does this, Theodor catches a glimpse of the front of his hoodie. And he's not at all surprised.

TWO WORDS, ONE FINGER is written in large capitals at the top, and below them is a picture of a green skeleton hand, with just that one finger out-stretched.

"What'ya got there?" continues the bully, who has now made it all the way over to the bench. "Let me see it for a sec, Salami. I'll be careful, promise."

Now Sammy looks up, and the sight of his face makes wrinkles shoot across Theodor's forehead.

The boy looks pale and scared. But he also looks brave. Like a soldier sitting in the back of a truck on the way to the front line, shaking off the nerves before it starts.

"No!" he says, loudly and commandingly while jumping up from the bench.

For a brief moment, the pack leader hesitates, and Theodor ponders if it might work. If the mere shock of facing resistance from an otherwise easy victim could actually be enough to make them change their minds.

But then he sees the leader intertwine his fingers and crack them with a sound that, despite the distance, reaches his ears clearly.

"WHAT DID YOU SAY, SALAMI?" he yells, but he doesn't give Sammy a chance to answer. Instead, he leaps forward and kicks his leg, so he falls sideways, landing back first on the bench seat.

Meanwhile, his two lackeys sneak in behind the bench and lean over its backrest.

With eerily rehearsed and synchronous moves—as such bullies unfortunately often have—they grab him. One of them by his leg, the other by his hair and his right arm.

Then they start poking, slapping, and pushing— three cowards taking turns—while the leader keeps repeating his rhetorical question over and over.

"WHAT DID YOU SAY, SAMMY SALAMI? WHAT DID YOU SAY? WHAT DID YOU SAY?"

Not on my fucking watch, Theodor thinks, throwing his cigarette on the ground. Next, he grabs the rims of the wheelchair and rolls it out from the smoking shelter and onto the tile walkway leading out to the road.

CHAPTER 13

"LEAVE HIM ALONE, YOU LITTLE WEASELS!"

These are the words with which Theodor decides to announce his arrival. Had he had more time to prepare—and had his blood been boiling a bit less—he might have fine-tuned a bit. He might have found a slightly more diplomatic synonym for the last word.

But Theodor Moody isn't exactly known for taking back his words once they've been uttered, and this time will be no exception either.

"What the fuck did you just say to us, old man?" the bully boss asks.

"I told you to leave him alone."

Above the edge of the hoodie with the green skeleton hand, the young man's head turns from side to side, as if he's scanning the area to determine if there is a hidden camera somewhere.

"Yes, it's you punks I'm talking to," Theodor says, and after a moment of reflection, he decides it probably won't change anything, so he adds, "Especially you, you little pissant."

"Fuck him, Alex," says one of the aspiring henchmen in the background. "He just came from the hospital. Probably just a crazy old dude. Or demented, like Bryan's grandma."

"I'm *not* demented," Theodor protests. "In fact, I've got an excellent memory. Especially when it comes to faces. So, if I had to, I could easily describe what you punks look like. I won't forget that anytime soon."

"Bullshit!" the boss bully says. "If you—"

"Especially yours," Theodor interrupts. "Was it Alex, they called you? Your mug and that classy shirt you're wearing have made quite an impression."

"Do you know this guy, Salami? Is it your fucking grandpa or something?"

On the bench, Sammy starts to shake his head, but Theodor sends him a look that makes him stop.

"Sammy and I aren't related," Theodor says. "But I know his mother very well. And if one day she should come and tell me that Sammy has had trouble with you again, I promise you that my memory will work just fine. Your faces have been stored, believe me."

"Alex, let's just get out of here," says the bully on the leader's left. "It ain't worth it."

But Alex doesn't agree with that notion. That much

is revealed by his icy eyes—and subsequently by his hand, which finds its way into the pocket of his hoodie. When it reappears, it's holding a pocketknife that he opens with a quick flick of his hand.

"Fuck, Alex. You can't just—"

"Shut your fucking mouth, Danny!" Alex snarls, fixing his gaze on Theodor as he tilts the knife back and forth in front of him. "Fucking old fart in a fucking wheelchair. Thinks he's all that, huh?"

He takes a step forward, and Theodor's hands instinctively move to the rims of the wheelchair and begin to pull them backward.

"Where do you think you're going, huh?"

"Take it easy, kid."

"You stuck? That it? Do you want me to give you a push?"

With those words, Alex lunges forward and kicks the armrest above the left wheel so that the seat tilts backward—while the wheelchair itself turns sideways.

A scorching sensation goes through Theodor's hands and shins as they meet the asphalt. A second later, the same pain continues up to his hip as his knees give way and let him fall helplessly onto his side.

His vision flickers, and spots of the same silver-white color as the blade of the knife in the bully's hand cover his field of view.

A school bully. A spoiled little shit who doesn't have

the brains to understand the consequences of his actions. Is that really how it's going to end?

Part of Theodor isn't particularly surprised. And not particularly sad either, for that matter. He has stayed alive mostly because he made a promise to his late wife ... but hey, surely, she can't be too disappointed by a departure like this. Him dying as a hero defending a little boy.

"Let him g-go, Alex! Or I'll call the police!"

What are you doing, kid? Theodor thinks as he looks up and sees the cleaning lady's boy, now standing with his bike between his legs and a cell phone in his hand.

The bully with the knife also turns around to look at the boy, but he doesn't seem worried about the threat. In fact, his voice sounds chirpy, almost as if he's excited at the thought of running from the cops when he says:

"I'll give you a ten-second head start, Salami."

It takes a moment for the words to sink in with Sammy, but when they do, his face turns almost as gray as the autumn sky above them.

"Alex, I ..."

"Ten ... nine ... eight," Alex begins, tilting the knife from side to side as if it were the pendulum of a metronome.

Sammy opens his mouth but then closes it again without saying anything and instead uses his energy to grab the bike's handlebars with both hands.

Then he starts pedaling.

On a bike in good condition, the remaining seven seconds might have been enough for Sammy to build up sufficient speed. But since some of the spokes in his rear wheel are still bent from being stomped on by Alex Skinner's right foot, the rear wheel wobbles, making it difficult for him to keep his balance.

A few seconds is all it takes for the two wannabe thugs to catch up with him and pull him off the bike.

"Keep him steady," Alex orders. Then he bends down close to Theodor and whispers: "Do you want me to give him an extra slash for you?"

Following that message, he turns his back on Theodor and starts walking toward his helpless victim.

No. He doesn't walk. He *strolls*. As if he were casually promenading on the beach, looking for rocks.

For some reason, that detail is infuriating to Theodor. If his damned legs didn't refuse to listen to him, there'd be hell to pay for those little pricks.

No further does Theodor get before a handful of pebbles start to tremble and then rise above the asphalt in a one-meter radius around him.

And a situation, already off the rails, becomes infinitely worse.

CHAPTER 14

It starts with the knife. It gets ripped out of Alex Skinner's hand with so much force that his arm is pulled backward—almost to the point where something could break. Next, it soars through the air, blade first, in the direction of the two hellions holding the cleaning lady's son.

Only barely does the knife miss the left bully's shoulder. In fact, it comes so close that Theodor can hear it stroking the sleeve of his jacket.

The knife's journey ends ten to twelve yards behind the three boys, where it burrows into the trunk of an old oak tree. So deep that getting it out will probably require tools.

The next thing Theodor registers, in this bizarre state of feeling simultaneously powerful and powerless, is Sammy's school bag.

Unlike the knife, the bag doesn't miss its target as it pulls free of the luggage rack of the overturned bike and flies through the air, carried by an invisible hand. It hits the aspiring mafia boss on his right thigh with such force that he is thrown sideways out onto the asphalt.

He tries to soften his fall with his hands. Though somewhat successful, the price is two torn-up palms that pull a couple of wide, bright red brushstrokes across the dark gray surface of the road.

Both Alex Skinner and his minions scream; him in pain, them in horror.

Next, the bike also lifts off the ground, and Theodor —now left only feeling powerless—tries to stop it. Tries to regain control over something of which he understands nothing except that he is to blame.

Take a deep breath, he orders himself. *Cool yourself down and you may be able to stop it.*

He tries ... but the bike doesn't care about his efforts, and behind it, the skateboard has also decided to join the party. Together they hang in the air, faintly vibrating as if gathering energy for a merciless launch.

"I ... can't ... control it," Theodor groans, first to himself and then to the terrified kids. "I can't control it. Run!"

For a split second, they all stare at him with the same uncomprehending look. Then the realization comes, and the two bullies let go of Sammy. Without looking back, they flee across the grass and into a wooded area farther on.

Behind him, Theodor hears their leader do the same —bolt with his tail between his legs—but he doesn't turn around to see it. His eyes are locked on the bike and skateboard, which now take off.

The bike hits the grass next to Sammy, digging a narrow ditch into it with one of its pedals, while the skateboard flies all the way over to the wooded area, where it collides with a tree and breaks in two with a loud snap.

After that sound, everything falls silent. If Theodor's own strained breathing is disregarded, that is. And Sammy's.

The boy sits on the grass. His blond hair is a tangled mess, and he looks exhausted.

Exhausted and utterly perplexed ... but not terrified anymore. He knows, just as Theodor does, that it's over. The bullies are not coming back now.

If ever.

You could have killed them.

The thought is his own, but it's Martha's voice Theodor imagines as he thinks it.

And she's right. He *could* have killed them.

He puts his hands on the road and pulls himself across the asphalt until he's close enough to the wheelchair to reach it.

With effort, he gets the seat flipped back up, but it

doesn't take many seconds for him to realize that the next step—getting his own body up there—is too much to handle.

"Let me help you," a bright voice says behind him.

Theodor turns his head and sees the cleaning lady's boy standing there with his hand outstretched.

For a moment, Theodor stares at that hand without saying anything. He's not keen on accepting it. And he's especially not keen on admitting that he *has to* accept it.

"Pull the brakes on the wheels first," he grumbles, nodding toward the wheelchair.

"These?"

Theodor nods, and the boy locks both wheels. Then he reaches out his hand again—and this time Theodor accepts it.

With the help of the kid, it's surprisingly easy, and after only two attempts, Theodor is back in the seat of his wheelchair.

He releases the brakes, rolls back and forth a few feet to check that everything is working, and then raises his head with the intention of saying thank you.

But the boy is no longer next to him. He has moved on to the next task. He's standing out on the grass, staring at his bike in despair. The chance of him being able to ride home on it now isn't exactly—

"GET AWAY FROM HIM!"

The voice is louder and harsher than the last time he heard it, so Theodor doesn't recognize it right away. It clicks into place, however, when the cleaning lady shouts again.

"I SAID, GET AWAY FROM HIM, SAMMY!"

"Mom, he didn't do anything," Sammy begins, but he's speaking to the deaf ears of a worried mother, and she doesn't hear a single word.

"OH MY GOD, SAMMY, WHAT HAPPENED?" she shouts, jumping off her own bike and running over to her son on the grass.

"I'm fine, Mom."

That's all he gets to say before his mother's attention is moved elsewhere. Specifically, to the elderly gentleman sitting in a wheelchair in the middle of the empty street.

"You!" she snarls. "You leave my son alone. Do you understand that, you crazy old freak? You leave my son alone and you leave me alone!"

"Mom, he hasn't—"

"Quiet, Sammy. We're going home. Now."

"But, Mom—"

"NOW, SAMMY! BRING YOUR BIKE AND YOUR BAG. WE'RE LEAVING!"

Sammy looks up at his mother in disbelief, then at Theodor, and then back at his mother. Then he shrugs and crouches down to pick up the bike. Once that's done, he grabs his bag from the sidewalk, puts his comic book into it, and attaches it to the bike.

Meanwhile, his mother keeps staring at Theodor.

She doesn't say anything, but her eyes promise that any attempt at communication will be met with the verbal equivalent of a nuclear bomb.

Therefore, Theodor remains silent. Not because he is particularly intimidated by her, but because he knows it would be a waste of time to try to have a sensible conversation with a woman as hysterical as she is right now.

"Good," she says when the boy is ready. "Now let's go."

From his seat in the wheelchair, Theodor watches them ride down the street—the mother in a straight line, the boy in a curvy one—until they turn left and disappear out of sight behind a tall building.

CHAPTER 15

As she sits at the kitchen table in her home an hour later, Yuki's hands are still shaking. However, it's for a different reason now. In fact, since the moment she left her workplace and spotted Sammy across the street, she has gone through three different phases, all of which made her fingers tremble.

Cause number one was the shock of seeing her son out on the grass, surrounded by his things, which had obviously been thrown around. Then came the anger when she realized that he was with the old freak from room 02. She assumed that he ... oh God, just the thought.

But she was wrong. Too quick to place the blame. She sees that now.

And therein lies the third reason. Her hands quiver at this moment, not with fear, not with anger, but with shame. Out of guilt for having yelled at Mr. Moody, who had apparently only tried to help her child. To save him from Alex Skinner and his goons.

Sammy sits across from her on the other side of the kitchen table. He's staring at her, she can sense that, but she's not quite ready to move her gaze from her own hands in her lap and meet his.

"I'm sorry, Sammy," she sighs. "You tried to explain to me what had happened, and I didn't listen."

"You were scared," Sammy says calmly. "I get that. I just felt bad for that man. The way you yelled at him."

You don't deserve him, she thinks. *You don't deserve a son this good. You know that, right?*

She lifts her head, meets his gaze, and smiles.

"I'll apologize to him tomorrow. He's one of the patients over at the rehabilitation center."

"Can I come along?"

"What? No, I don't think that's a good idea."

"Why not?"

Yuki hesitates for a moment and then shrugs.

"Mr. Moody is ..."

Rude, prejudiced, coarse, awkward, racist, condescending, bitter.

"... a very private person. Doesn't like too many visitors, you know."

"But I just want to thank him."

"I can do that for you."

Sammy grimaces and tilts his head.

"I'd ... also like to talk to him."

"About what?"

"Well, I don't know. Just talk a bit, I guess," Sammy says, and again his face has that strange expression. As if he's taken a bite of a vegetable he doesn't like.

All of a sudden, it dawns on Yuki: Her son may have left out some details in his description of the events.

"Sammy," she says, leaning forward so she can put her hand over his on the table. "Explain to me one more time why it was that Alex and the others ran off?"

Sammy looks at her and bites his lip.

"I told you," he says. "The man in the wheelchair said he'd call the police and tell them what they looked like if they didn't stop."

"Uh-huh," Yuki says, nodding slowly. "But that wasn't all he did, was it?"

For a long time, Sammy does nothing but chew on his lower lip, staring at her uncertainly. But then the dam suddenly bursts, and the words come pouring out.

"He's a freaking superhero, Mom! Like Professor X or something. He ... he didn't touch anything at all, and then things just started flying. The bike and the bag and the skateboard, it all just floated up in the air and then he fired it at them."

"At Alex and the others?"

"Yeah. He hit Alex with the bag, and then the other two ran into the woods, and ..."

He stops mid-sentence and squints.

"Why aren't you more surprised?" he asks. "I said he made things *fly*."

Yuki gives his hand a gentle squeeze and strokes her thumb over it a few times.

"Sammy, I ... I've seen him do something similar. Over at the center."

"Cool," the boy mutters.

"No, Sammy. Not cool. Scary. That's what it is. Scary and dangerous. And whatever it is, he can't control it."

"I know," Sammy says, nodding thoughtfully. "He couldn't control it today either. But maybe he can learn."

"Sammy, no."

"Come on, Mom. I just want to talk to him."

Yuki takes a breath and holds the air in her lungs as she stares at her son.

At his puppy eyes.

"We'll see, okay?" she says when the air can't be contained anymore. "It's not a promise!"

"Thanks, Mom."

"Don't you *thanks, Mom* me. I told you that it's not a promise."

"I know, I know. But still."

Yuki rolls her eyes but says nothing. Instead, she gets up from the table, finds some bread and a jar of peanut butter, and starts making a sandwich.

She's only halfway done when she stiffens and feels the butter knife slip out of her hand.

A truck engine in the driveway. Dean is home.

With her pulse pounding in her temples, she spins on her heels.

"Your bike," she says. "Where did you put it?"

"In the garage," Sammy replies, staring at her in confusion. "I put it in the garage like I always do."

"Stay here," she says, trying to sound calm. Then she runs out of the kitchen and down the hallway leading to the garage.

The garage, which also serves as a shed for their garden tools, has two entrances; a door that opens from inside the house, and a gate, large enough for the pickup truck, that opens with a remote.

Dean must have just pressed its button because she can hear the gate opening—and when she enters the garage, she can also see a wide square of light growing bigger and bigger on the floor.

"Come on, come on," she rushes herself as she puts her hands on the handles of the bike and drags it with her.

Her plan? To get it tucked away behind the old bookcase in the back of the garage before Dean spots it. Because if he sees what it looks like, he will start asking questions.

The race is on, and the light on the floor quickly approaches her heels as she struggles to steer the bike free of a stack of cardboard boxes and a rolled-up garden hose on the floor.

Victory is within reach, and she can almost taste it ...

but then the left side of the handlebars knocks against the edge of the bookcase.

The handlebar turns sideways. Below it, the front wheel does the same, and a split second later the bike rolls backward, while Yuki herself stumbles forward.

She regains her balance by letting go of the handles and letting the bike fall to the ground—along with the hope of her victory.

Because now, she has been caught by the light, and like a deer on the roads at night, she is unable to move away from it.

CHAPTER 16

"What the hell are you doing?" Dean asks as he gets out of the truck.

Yuki shrugs and attempts to put on her robot smile, but she can't even do that. It ends up as nothing more than an awkward grimace.

"I figured I'd clean up out here. It's long overdue."

Dean stares at her. Then he slams the truck door. Hard.

"And now the truth, please. I'm a cop. I can smell bullshit from a mile away. You know that."

"But it *is* the truth," Yuki says. "We've got so much junk out here that it's almost impossible to—"

"Why are you still wearing your work clothes?"

Horrified, Yuki looks down at herself. Then she wipes her damp palms on her apron and puts a loose tuft of hair back in place behind her ear.

"I-I'm sorry. I got so caught up in this that I completely—"

"You're *home* now, Yuki. Not at work. At this time of day, you're *a wife*. That's your job. And wives wear proper clothes. Pretty dresses so their husbands have something nice to look at. Hell, there'd be no new kids born otherwise. Who'd want to ruffle up someone parading around in ugly old work clothes like that?"

"Right, of course, Dean," she says, shaking her head. It's best to just agree with him when he lays a philosophy like that on the table.

"Besides, if I wanted a cleaning lady waltzing around at home, I probably would have bought me a little Mexican *señorita*. They're much cheaper. Now, show me that fucking bike."

He weaves in the last sentence without his voice changing in the least, and it takes a moment before Yuki even realizes what he said.

But as the words get through to her, she feels a chill crawl up her spine.

Aware that she only has the time it takes to pick up the bike to come up with a good story, she bends down.

"I-it was an accident," she says, closing her shaking fingers around the handles. "Actually, it was my fault. I wasn't thinking."

Not a bad start, if she has to say so herself. If there's one thing you can always count on, it's Dean agreeing that his wife is completely useless. Dumb as a goose.

"Can't say I'm surprised," he says. "What happened?"

"We had to turn at an intersection on the way home and I didn't check properly, so I pulled in, right in front of Sammy. He tried to get around me, of course, and, um, that's when he crashed into a bench."

"Into a bench? With the rear wheel? How exactly does that happen?"

"He ... he toppled over, of course," Yuki hastens to add, trying to suppress nervous laughter. "He didn't just *drive* into it. It wouldn't make sense that he could do that with the rear wheel first. The bike fell down on the bench, obviously."

Dean grabs her arm and squeezes it so hard that it feels like the skin is burning. It's scary how calculating he is. Even now, when his anger is spontaneous, he makes sure to grab above the place where her sleeves are rolled up to.

"It's a great story," he whispers through clenched teeth. "What do you say we pop into the house and see if Sammy remembers it that way too?"

"Dean, I—"

"And I think he should tell it all by himself, without you interfering. Isn't that a good idea?"

She doesn't give an answer, nor does he wait to get one. He just drags her with him toward the kitchen, where he stops in front of the door to send her one last reminder—in the shape of an icy stare—that she had better keep her mouth shut if she knows what's best for her. And only when he's received a nod from her does he enter.

"Hi, Sammy," he says in a friendly voice that is nothing like the one he used out in the garage. "How was school?"

"Hi, Dad. Yeah, it was okay."

"I see that your bike is not doing too well."

Sammy, who was chewing a piece of his peanut butter sandwich, freezes in place.

"What happened to it?" Dean continues as he walks over to the table, lays his hands on the boy's shoulders, and starts massaging them.

"I don't know, Dad. It was like that when I came out of school. I didn't see who did it."

"Aha," Dean says, glancing at Yuki. "That's too bad. Maybe I should come with you to school tomorrow? Talk to them as a cop, you know. See if anyone knows anything."

"I don't think that will help, Dad. All of us were inside, in the classrooms."

"Hm, yeah, I see," Dean says, his eyes still locked on his wife. "There's just one little thing that I don't quite get."

The boy looks up at him with uncertain eyes but says nothing.

"You see, Mom said you fell off your bike on the way home."

Silence.

"I ... yeah, I did. I just didn't want to say anything because I was afraid that you'd ..."

"That I'd what? Get mad?"

The boy shrugs.

"I only get mad if someone lies to me," Dean says. "Isn't that right, Mom?"

Now *that* is the lie of the century. You could wake Yuki up at shit o'clock at night to quiz her on that topic, and she could easily name twenty other things that will instantly trigger Dean's rage.

Still, she nods and smiles as Sammy looks at her to confirm his father's words.

Now Dean speaks again—and once more his tone of voice has changed completely. This time, his voice is pulled down to a deep, almost guttural pitch.

"So, I'll ask you one more time, Sammy. What happened to your bike?"

Yuki opens her mouth, but Dean shuts it again with a glance.

"It was some of the big kids from school who did it. They knocked it over and kicked it."

"Oh, yeah? Then what did you do?"

"What do you mean?"

Dean looks at him as if it's the most stupid thing he's heard in his life.

"They kicked your bike," he says. "So, what did you do to them?"

"I ... um, they're a lot bigger than me. And there were three of them."

Dean closes his eyes and slowly shakes his head. Then he leans closer to the boy.

"Listen, Sammy. You're a Rowley. That means you never let anyone step on you. And if someone does, you pay them back immediately."

"But, Dad—"

"It's the only way to deal with bullies like them. Speak their own language next time. They hit you, you hit harder. Got it?"

More silence.

"Got it?" repeats Dean, and under his big hands, Sammy's shoulders twitch.

"Okay, Dad, but ..."

"But what?"

"I don't think there will be a next time."

"And why is that?"

"There was a man who helped me."

With a glance, Dean sends his next question over to Yuki.

"It was an old man who is staying at the rehabilitation center," she says.

Again, Dean's face contracts in disappointment.

"So, my son needed help from some old man? Where was your mother?"

"I hadn't gotten off work yet," Yuki says, clearing her

throat. "Someone knocked over a pot of coffee in the common room, so I had to clean that up before I left."

"See, that's why women shouldn't work, Sammy," Dean says, patting his son on the shoulder. "Their children are left to fend for themselves."

Yuki can't follow his logic, but she doesn't try very hard either. She knows that Dean seizes every chance to point out that women ought to stay within arm's reach of the oven and the vacuum cleaner.

"By the way, Sammy. I've been thinking," Dean says, again in that deep, halfway-growling voice. "Shouldn't we take you over to Grandma and Grandpa's tonight? I think Grandpa wants to show you his new garden tractor. Then I can help Mom clean up the garage in the meantime. She really wants that done. Isn't that right, hon?"

Tears well up in Yuki's eyes, but she hides them with her hand, pretending to scratch her forehead as she mumbles:

"Yeah, that's true. It's such a mess out there."

"Exactly," Dean says, displaying his teeth in a predatory smile. "And also, we've got something we need to talk about, your mom and me."

PART IV
AN ODD COUPLE

"Don't let aging get you down.
It's too hard to get back up!"

Things that Martha used to say

CHAPTER 17

Dean really had something on his mind. A lot he wanted to *talk about*. So much, in fact, that it takes a full three days before Yuki is able to go back to work.

All things considered, it's going okay. Only a few times is it necessary for her to find a quiet corner and sit down until the pain in her hip has subsided.

Although her stomach is covered with bruises, it's her hip that hurts the most this time. It got a sprain when, during their *serious talk*, Dean decided to clarify a point with a visual element.

In other words, he twisted one of her arms around her back and pushed her halfway out over the railing on the first floor so she could see all the way down to the living room floor—while whispering in her ear that he ought to throw her down there.

And at that moment, when her husband—the all-

American hero who had once rescued her from a shipping container—threatened to let her fall, Yuki felt something give way in her hip as it pressed against the railing.

She probably ought to see a doctor about it, but obviously, that will have to wait until Dean's abstract painting on her stomach has faded.

Besides, it's neither Dean nor her sore hip that worries Yuki the most right now. What occupies her mind is the cleaning job.

Doing it. Keeping it.

Several times during the day, Yuki has heard the sound of high heels, and she knows that McKinney regularly patrols the corridors of the rehabilitation center. So, at some point, that sound is bound to come her way. And then, the final verdict is in.

In the late afternoon, it happens. About an hour before she's off work, McKinney tip-taps over to her—and even before she's opened her mouth, Yuki knows what's coming.

"Yuki, can I talk to you in my office?"

"If it's because I wasn't at work, then I can explain it."

"I really think we ought to go into my office, Yuki. Please come with me, okay?"

"Oh, okay," Yuki sighs, putting down the mop. "Of course."

The walk down the corridor feels much longer than

usual. And finite. As if they were moving through the dark and damp tunnels of the Roman catacombs. And as if there's a dark and cold stone cell awaiting her at the end.

Which isn't that far from the truth.

"Take a seat," McKinney says when they've entered her office an eternity later.

The office isn't very big, and usually, the manager's chair is the only one in there. Today, however, there is another chair on the other side of the table.

Yuki sits down, straightens her work apron, and then places her hands on her thighs because she doesn't know what else to do with them.

"We both know what this is about," McKinney begins. "So, I don't want to make it worse by drawing it out."

"Ms. McKinney, I'm really, *really* sorry," Yuki starts, but it doesn't even look like the words make it to the other side of the table. McKinney is completely caught up in her own agenda.

"Not even a week has passed since the two of us had a chat about this," she says, letting her hands fall to the sides in resignation. "I told you it would be the final warning. Since then, you've been away from work for three days. *Three* days, Yuki!"

Yuki lets her head fall forward and nods but says nothing.

"Trust me," McKinney continues. "I hate being in this

situation just as much as you do. But you've left me no choice."

She hesitates for a moment, running her big, rough farmer's hands back and forth along the edge of the desk.

Yuki uses the same pause to take a deep breath, tighten her stomach, and prepare for the next words from her boss's mouth.

It makes no real difference. It still hits her in the diaphragm as if it were one of Dean's fists.

"We have to say goodbye to you, Yuki. So, this is your notice ..."

McKinney says something more, a whole lot, actually, but Yuki has stopped listening. Her brain has received the primary message, and now it focuses on something else. On painting a picture for her. A picture of her, sitting in her prison at home, while the money in the matchbox under the washing machine—and the dream of freedom they represent—slowly rots away. Turns to dust. Just like her.

She jolts as McKinney's hand brushes hers, and she pulls it away as if she has touched something burning hot.

"Oh, sorry," McKinney says. "I didn't mean to startle you."

"It's okay, Ms. McKinney," Yuki replies, attempting to smile. "It's just a lot to swallow."

"Yes, of course. That's completely normal, but, um ... you do understand what I'm saying to you, right?"

Yuki makes another attempt to pull her lips up in a smile as she nods—and fails once more. In turn, tears start rolling down her cheeks. At least, that ought to answer the question. She wouldn't cry if she didn't understand, now, would she?

"Like I said, you have two weeks' notice," McKinney says, looking at her decisively. "But no one will bat an eye if you decide to take a couple of days to recover."

"I'll do my job," Yuki says, wiping her eyes.

McKinney nods and smiles.

"That's up to you. And if you want the rest of the day off, that's okay too."

"That won't be necessary," Yuki says. "Sammy and I bike home together. Besides, I promised him that we could visit Mr. Moody when I get off work."

"Mr. Moody? The older gentleman in 02?"

Yuki nods.

"Why on earth would you ..." McKinney starts, but then she cuts herself off and shakes her head. "Sorry, that's none of my business. Just promise you'll let me know if you need a day off ... or if you need someone to talk to. Okay?"

Yuki smiles and nods again. Then she grabs the armrests of the chair, preparing to get up, while looking questioningly at her boss.

McKinney blinks her eyes slowly and makes a *sure, go ahead* motion with her hand.

After entering the corridor, Yuki goes back to where she left her cleaning cart—but she doesn't stop when she's reached it. She continues past it, all the way down to the end, where she opens a door and steps outside.

On this side of the rehabilitation center is a small, Japanese garden that the resident guests can use freely. In the center of it is a large gravel bed, filled with light gray pebbles, raked in a figure-eight pattern.

Many times, especially after realizing she was only eight months away from her goal, she's sat there staring at that figure eight. Dreaming of the future.

Today, it's not the number eight she sees. Today, it's the horizontal twin of the number.

The infinity sign.

And realizing that makes her burst into tears.

CHAPTER 18

Torture. Gross mistreatment of innocent, often elderly people. That's what it is. And the sadists probably get a big, fat hourly wage for it. It wouldn't surprise him in the slightest.

But despite his defiance—and the death stares he gives the young physiotherapist every time he bosses him around—Theodor has to admit that the scoundrel must be doing something right.

Because there *is* progress. He's not completely free of the wheelchair yet, but he can walk much farther without losing his balance. So, no more calling the nurse when his bladder needs to be emptied. Now he can walk to the john himself and handle things.

"Nice work today, Mr. Moody," the sadist says as he closes the zipper of his red torture bag and walks toward the doorway. "See you tomorrow."

"Mm," Theodor grumbles, not hiding the fact that his enthusiasm at that prospect isn't exactly overwhelming.

As soon as the young man is out the door, Theodor sits down on the edge of the bed, letting out a heavy sigh. He is exhausted—because despite his passive-aggressive facade, he does try to follow the physiotherapist's instructions as best as possible. He bends and stretches like a madman, hoping that he'll soon be able to avoid staring at the walls of this drab room.

You probably won't even recognize the house when you get home, he thinks—and smiles when a new thought, an inner image, follows in its wake:

His neighbor, Mary-Lou Watson, who must be on the verge of a breakdown about now because his lawn looks like a wilderness. Perhaps she'll end up getting so desperate that she sneaks over to mow it herself.

In Theodor's eyes, this image is quite entertaining, and he doesn't just smile now. He chuckles.

"Mr. Moody?"

Theodor stiffens and looks toward the door, where he spots the cleaning lady.

After spending a second reading the expression in her eyes—embarrassment, not anger—he narrows his own.

"Have you come to yell at me again?"

The cleaning lady winces and rubs her arm as she looks downward. Then she steps over the threshold.

A movement behind her makes Theodor aware that she is not alone. Her boy is with her. He is standing in the hallway with his hands folded and a face as uncomfortable as his mother's.

"I've come to apologize," the cleaning lady says. "I shouldn't have yelled at you."

Theodor ignores her and instead makes eye contact with her son.

"Are you going to stand out there cowering all day, kid?"

Theodor knows that he has heard the boy's name, but right now all he can remember is the nickname that the bullies used, *salami*. And that probably wouldn't go down too well.

The boy doesn't say a word. His mother, on the other hand, does.

"You were trying to help, but I didn't know that at the time, and ... I overreacted. I'm really sorry about that."

Now she has gotten Theodor's attention. He shifts his gaze from the boy to his mother's eyes.

"What a load of bullcrap," he says, meaning it wholeheartedly. "You didn't *overreact*."

"Sorry, what?"

"I don't know what it's like in China," Theodor continues. "But in this country, we protect our children. Your son looked to be in trouble, and he was in the company of a complete stranger. I'd be a lot more worried if you hadn't blown a fuse."

For a few long seconds, his words are left hanging in the air while the cleaning lady's face works its way through a palette of different expressions. Confusion turns into indignation, which turns into disbelief, and from there moves into a strange, almost compassionate expression.

"Um, yeah, I guess," she says, taking a few steps closer, signaling her son to follow.

When the boy has reached her, the cleaning lady pulls something out of the pocket of her apron and hands it to Theodor.

"We ... um, we've brought you a little something. To say thanks."

Theodor stares at the little, wrapped box in her hands with such condemnation that you'd think it was a tarantula she was trying to hand him. Then he turns his face away.

"Keep it. I don't want it."

"But ... you don't even know what it is!"

"Don't need to. I don't want a gift. It's not necessary. Besides, I probably won't even like ... whatever that stuff is."

The cleaning lady's face once again flickers through a series of different expressions. This time the wheel of fortune stops somewhere between disbelief and indignation.

"Whatever that stuff is?" she repeats. "What exactly do you think is in this, Mr. Moody?"

"Well, how should I know?" Theodor mutters. "Raw fish or noodles, maybe. You hear so much."

Awkward silence. Then the cleaning lady lets out an involuntary sputtering chuckle and rubs her hand over her cheek.

In general, Theodor Moody doesn't like anyone laughing at him, and normally he'd have his defensive walls up immediately. Yet, something makes him hesitate this time and suppress the urge to ask her what the hell is so funny.

Her eyes. It's them. They don't follow suit, although the lips are smiling. Instead, they look sad. Like she's about to break down somewhere in there, behind the facade.

"It's chocolate, Mr. Moody," she says as the chuckle dies out. "Good, old-fashioned chocolate. And if you don't want to eat it, you don't have to, but it's important to us that we say thank you."

Theodor stares at her and then glances down at her son.

Under the disheveled, blond bangs, the kid's brown eyes look uncertain. That's no wonder, though, considering what happened the last time they saw each other. But the boy maintains eye contact, and for that, Theodor respects him.

"Put it on the table," he sighs, making a sweeping motion with his hand. "But for the record, I still think it's nonsense."

The cleaning lady gives him a gentle smile and then places the box on the bedside table. Meanwhile, Theodor leans to the side and looks out the window.

"Have you fixed it?"

"Fixed what?"

"The bike. I don't see it out there."

Mother and son exchange a look which answers the question for Theodor even before she opens her mouth and puts it into words.

"No, we ... we haven't had time to look at it yet. So, we just get up a bit earlier in the morning and walk to school instead. It's no big deal."

She strokes a hand over her son's shoulder and smiles at him.

"Isn't that right, Sammy?"

Sammy! That was it! Of course. Sammy Salami.

"Sure, Mom."

Theodor raises one eyebrow and stares at the boy.

"Can't your dad fix it?"

"Um, yeah ... I think so. When he gets the time."

"When he gets the time?" Theodor grumbles. "We're talking about a handful of bent spokes on a rear wheel. How much time does he need?"

No answer, neither from mother nor son ... which can only mean that the kid's dad is either a lazy couch potato or a white-collar worker afraid of getting his hands dirty, like Kevin.

"Here's the deal, kid," Theodor says. "Bring it over here tomorrow and I'll help you fix it."

"That's very kind of you, Mr. Moody," the cleaning lady says. "But I don't think it's a good idea."

"Of course it is. It's an excellent idea. There's no reason for the kid to keep walking to school when it's such a little thing."

He points his index finger at Sammy.

"Does your dad have any tools at home?"

Sammy nods.

"And do you know what an adjustable wrench is?"

Sammy nods again.

"Good. Then you bring one of those. The biggest you can find. Deal?"

This time, the boy looks hesitantly up at his mother, and not until she nods—after a very long period of reflection—does he do the same.

CHAPTER 19

At a quarter past four the following afternoon, the boy comes, dragging his bicycle across the lawn in front of the rehabilitation center, and stops at the smoking shelter where Theodor is sitting.

"Hi, Mr. Moody."

Theodor responds with a nod and a short humming sound.

"The wrench?"

"In the bag," Sammy says, smiling as he leans his bike against one wall of the shelter and starts rummaging through the school bag on its luggage rack.

"Not there!" Theodor snaps.

Sammy looks up at him in confusion and then down at the wrench he has just pulled out of his bag.

"The bike," Theodor elaborates. "It's a plexiglass wall. If you lean the bike against it, you'll scratch the glass."

"O-oh, okay, I'm sorry," Sammy stutters, quickly pulling the bike away from the wall and laying it on the grass. "Is this okay?"

Theodor nods and then rolls the wheelchair closer to the bike.

After studying its rear wheel for a moment, he nods to himself and signals the boy to get the wrench. But when Sammy tries to hand it to him, Theodor simply shakes his head.

"I said I would help you. Not that I would do it for you."

The boy stares at him skeptically, as if trying to figure out if it's a joke. Then he shrugs and squats down next to the bike.

"Do you see those little screw gizmos at the top?" Theodor asks.

"These?"

"Yeah. They're called *nipples*. We need to loosen them first. Normally you would use a nipple wrench, but I didn't think you'd know what that was. So, we'll use the wrench instead."

"Yeah, I didn't know," the boy admits with a smile and a shrug.

"Start by unscrewing those three," Theodor says, and as Sammy starts working, he glances toward the building behind them. "Where's your mother?"

"She'll come later. She had to pick up a package before the post office closes. Is this good?"

"A little looser."

Sammy nods and goes back to work with pursed lips. He looks deeply focused ... although Theodor has noticed that the boy glances at him every time he looks away.

"Go ahead and ask."

"Sorry?" Sammy says, pulling on a mask of almost comical innocence.

"You've got something you wanna ask me," Theodor elaborates. "So, go ahead and do it."

Sammy hesitates, takes a deep breath, hesitates a little more—and then it comes gushing out:

"How did you do it? When you made the bike fly and scared Alex and the others away. It was completely insane!"

"On that, we can agree," Theodor says. "It was *very* insane. But as for *how* it happened ..."

He finishes the sentence by shrugging his shoulders.

The lack of explanation doesn't seem to discourage the kid, though. Quite the contrary.

"I've been thinking about it," he says. "And I can only see three options."

"Is that so? Well, do tell."

"Alien, mutant, or magician."

Theodor frowns but still makes a *do go on* gesture with his hand.

"You have telekinesis, right?" Sammy says. "And in

comics and movies, it's always one of those three things that's the explanation."

"Nonsense," Theodor quips. "I'm from Pennsylvania, kid. Not from Mars."

"That's not what I ... oh, never mind. Is it something you've always been able to do?"

Theodor shakes his head.

"Nope, it's only happened three times—all within the last few weeks. I think they're loose enough now. Next, we need to get the spokes straightened. You do that by taking them one at a time and holding the wrench behind them while pressing at the top and bottom."

"Like this?"

"No, vertically."

"Oh, okay. Like this then?"

"Exactly."

"So, you can't control it at all?"

"No."

"Have you tried? Like, for real."

Although Theodor doesn't really need to think about the answer, he hesitates for a while before giving it. Because yes, he has tried, several times over the last few weeks, to repeat it, but he's not sure it's a good idea to involve the kid in all of this.

"I've tried a couple of times, yeah," he ends up saying. "No luck."

Sammy nods thoughtfully and moves the wrench to the next spoke on the rear wheel.

"And what do the doctors say?"

"About what?"

"About your superpowers. What do they think it is?"

"Nothing. I haven't told any doctors—and I have no intention of doing so."

"Why not?"

Theodor tilts his head, giving the boy a *you can't be serious* look.

"I'm not going to be their guinea pig and get ... poked all over. I'm too old for that."

Sammy lets out a chuckle and shakes his head.

"That's exactly what my mom thought you would say."

Theodor doesn't answer. He just frowns and pretends to spot something over in the woods on the other side. His hope is that it will provoke a pause with the boy's bombardment of questions.

It works ... but only for about twenty seconds.

"Were you also ... angry the other times?"

"What do you mean?"

"In a lot of my comics, it's when the heroes get angry that they can use their powers."

"This isn't a comic book, kid."

"No, no, I know. Were you, though?"

Theodor squints his eyes and sighs. But that's not enough for Sammy, who keeps staring at him.

"Maybe I was," he finally grumbles.

A cryptic smile appears on Sammy's lips. He pulls the wrench away from the spokes of the rear wheel and dumps it onto the grass in front of Theodor's feet.

"Lift this."

"Kid ..."

"Do it," Sammy insists. "Think of what made you angry the first time and then lift it."

"I can think of something that's starting to piss me off right now. Will that work?"

"Come on, humor me."

"This is ridiculous," Theodor grunts. Still, there is a part of him that feels the boy may be on to something. And with that realization, two images appear before his mind's eye.

The first is of the center flower in the bouquet that his heartless and brainless daughter-in-law gave him; the pink orchid.

The second picture is of Kevin. Theodor's own flesh and blood, but in a completely different wrapping. A custom-tailored Armani wrapping and a chronic business smile so false that it could be a tacked-on piece of garment. Kevin holding the damned brochure for the Ridgeview Care Center in his hand.

Care center. Fancy words for a place to stow away your parents, as if they were cardboard boxes with stuff you can't quite bring yourself to throw out and therefore hide away in a dusty attic.

The sound of a shocked gasp interrupts his stream of thought, and when he realizes what triggered it, he lets out one himself.

The boy sits cross-legged on the grass, his eyes wide open, one hand covering his mouth. In front of him, about ten inches above the ground, the wrench hangs in the air, spinning around itself in slow circles.

"Holy s-shit, I didn't really think it would work," the boy mutters between his fingers. "It's flying, Mr. Moody. *It's flying!*"

The excitement in his voice is so pure, so *untamed*, that it's hard for Theodor not to be infected by it.

A second later, it's over. The wrench falls onto the grass with a thump and stays there, completely still.

"That was so cool," Sammy mutters. "Do it again!"

Theodor shakes his head and points to the bike.

"No more monkey business. We need to get that bike fixed."

"But—"

"No buts. You want it to be ready when your mom comes, right?"

"Yeah, but it—"

"Then get to work."

Sammy tightens his lips and stares at him defiantly for a moment but then gives up and grabs the wrench.

Somewhere below the surface, Theodor feels a bit sorry for the kid. After all, he gets why he's fascinated by all this. And truth be told, Theodor feels some of the same childlike wonder and curiosity.

But beneath that place, further down in the depths of his consciousness, there are stronger emotions. The fear of the unknown. The fear that it will get out of control again, as it did with the bullies the other day.

And not least, the fear that none of it is real. That he never actually woke up after he collapsed on the gravel in front of the community house. That he could be lying in a hospital bed, hooked up to a respirator, dreaming it all.

"Looks good, Sammy," says a woman's voice behind them. "Maybe you should be a bike mechanic when you grow up."

"Astronaut," the boy replies without looking up. "How many times do I have to tell you, Mom?"

The cleaning lady lets out a dry laugh that gives Theodor the same feeling as the day before: that something is weighing her down. Something she struggles to keep locked away behind the smiling facade.

"Has he been good?" she asks, coming up to the side of Theodor's wheelchair, but before he can answer, Sammy preempts him:

"Well, he's behaved okay. He forced me into child labor ... but other than that, okay."

"Samuel Rowley!" bursts out of the cleaning lady. Then she—embarrassed and not without fear—glances at Theodor, awaiting his reaction.

147

"He's not the worst helper in the world," Theodor says. "His thumbs point the right way, and his head is screwed on properly. However, his attitude could use a little adjustment. You, being his mother, should know that."

For a few seconds, the watchful expression lingers on the cleaning lady's face as she tilts her head and stares at the man in the wheelchair as if he were a penguin in a desert.

Then the penguin's lips form a rare smile, and she, visibly relieved, buries her face in her hands and laughs.

"You sure got me there, Mr. Moody. I didn't know what to say."

Theodor nods, *oh, I know*, then turns his attention to Sammy.

"How does it look, kid?"

"Almost done. I just need to tighten this, and ... there. Done."

"Let me check," Theodor says, holding out his hand.

The boy picks up the bike, rolls it over to the wheelchair, and waits patiently while Theodor grabs the spokes and pulls them, one by one.

"Not bad," he says. "Not bad at all. Try taking it for a test spin on the grass. And wipe off that smug grin. It was a bike wheel you fixed. Not a jet engine."

Sammy doesn't wipe off his grin. If anything, it gets wider when he mounts the bike, steps on the pedals, and discovers that it rides flawlessly.

"Thank you, Mr. Moody," the cleaning lady says as her son goes around them in large circles. "You don't know how much it means to us."

Theodor opens his mouth, intending to make a half-witted comment that she'd better not show up with a gift this time, neither raw fish nor chocolate ... but when he lifts his head and sees her, he changes his mind.

Her eyes are wet. Whatever she keeps locked away in there can't be contained much longer.

Even though he tries to tell himself that it's nonsense —that he barely knows her—it pains Theodor a bit to see her like that. He just doesn't know what to do about it. That kind of stuff, talking about feelings and comforting, was Martha's area of expertise when she was alive. He's much better at putting up shelves and straightening spokes on bicycle wheels.

But Martha isn't here anymore, so he'll just have to do his best.

"You're welcome," he says. "He's a good kid, that boy of yours."

CHAPTER 20

Like a doomsday clock, where every day the hour hand counts down toward a night that will never end once it has begun.

That's how the days feel for Yuki during this period, and it's only getting worse, given that all her attempts at finding a new job have been in vain.

Also, she hasn't told Dean about the firing yet. One thing, of course, is that she expects he'll want one of his *serious talks* with her when it happens. But that's not even what she fears the most.

No, Yuki's biggest concern is that Dean will force her to stay at home. That he'll rob her of the opportunity to keep putting money aside—and to send money to her family in Thailand, as she usually does.

You could do it now. You could push the cart away, pick Sammy up early from school, get the money that's in the matchbox, and just leave. It would be tough, but it has to be possible.

Ludicrous. A naive idea that would never work. Because she has done her calculations, made her detailed plans, and analyzed them, looking for possible holes.

And a meticulous analysis is necessary. Because Dean isn't just a ruthless man. He is a ruthless *policeman*. An experienced manhunter with all the tips, tricks, and connections of the police force at his disposal.

And once he's set his mind on something, Dean won't give up. So, there is no point in an impulsive and half-hearted solution. She needs a new identity, Sammy needs a new identity, and they have to hide in a place where he can't find them.

That kind of thing costs money, specifically, the usual quarter of her income for the next eight months. But in a week, she no longer has an income.

"Now you've dusted off the same spot three times," she hears behind her. "I thought Asians were supposed to be efficient and hard-working."

"Big words from a man who's been sitting on his ass since the day I met him," she replies, turning her head toward the armchair to make sure Mr. Moody can see her rolling her eyes. And that she's not in the mood for a game of racist ping-pong today. Of course, this goes completely over his head.

"Mm, sad but true," he says, sighing. "Bed, wheelchair, toilet, smoking shelter ... and then back to start. It's driving me nuts."

Hoping her silence will clue him in, Yuki doesn't answer. But apparently, he's in a chatty mood today.

"I can't wait to get out of here," he continues. "How you can stand to trot around here every single day is a mystery to me."

Yuki closes her eyes and bites her lip for a moment. Then she takes a breath, turns to him, and says:

"You forget that we have our wonderful patients keeping us company."

"No need to get wise," he replies, looking out the window. "By the way, how is it going with your kid's bike?"

"Fine."

One-syllable answers. Surely that must give him a hint.

"So, it doesn't wobble anymore?"

Nope, there is no stopping him today. You'll need to spell it out if you want to get through to him.

"No, it's riding smoothly. Listen, Mr. Moody, I've had a couple of hard days at home, so if it's okay with you, I'd prefer—"

"That's good. The poor kid had enough to deal with as it was, and then losing his bike on top of it all ..."

"What's that supposed to mean?"

Theodor hesitates and gives her a confused stare. At the corners of his mouth, an uncertain smile flickers.

"What's that supposed to mean?" Yuki repeats.

"I, um ... what?"

"That my son had enough to deal with. What did you mean by that?"

"Well, nothing. I just think he has obviously had problems with those bullies for a while, and it can't have been easy. But now it's been dealt with, so—"

"And you don't think it's been *dealt with* before? You think I just ignored it?"

Theodor doesn't answer. He just stares at her with the same confused expression as he had earlier. And for some reason, that angers Yuki.

"Let me tell you something, Mr. Moody," she says. "That little pissant, Alex Skinner, has been on my son's back for a *long* time and I've tried *everything* to make it stop. I've talked to all his teachers, to the principal, to the Skinner kid's parents. I even spoke to the janitor, and none of it helped."

No response. Not that he would have had time to give one.

"So, I'm not going to stand here and let you talk to me like that. Sammy is *my* son and I'll take care of him, thank you very much."

The old man in the armchair still doesn't say a word. However, there is a voice in the back of Yuki's mind that does. The voice of her guilty conscience ... which today sounds an awful lot like Dean's voice.

And how are you planning to do that when you don't have a job anymore?

"I'll take care of him," she repeats, but the words no longer have any power behind them, and they come out of her mouth so muffled that she can barely even hear them herself. "I'm his mother. It's my responsibility to take care of him."

Only now, as the taste of salt hits the corner of her mouth and then spreads out onto her tongue, does Yuki realize that she is crying.

Her hands are also trembling. So much so that she almost drops the dust cloth when she puts it down on the windowsill.

"Please excuse me, I need a moment," she stutters as she walks toward the door, embarrassed and beaten. But when she puts her hand on its handle, something makes her hesitate.

"I ... I was just told that I don't have my job anymore," she says. "And it was a bit of a hit because I ... *we* badly need the money."

She looks up at him, waiting for a reaction that doesn't come. He just sits there, reclining in his soft armchair, staring blankly at her. And for a moment, even though she knows it's not fair, she hates him for it.

"Nothing?" she asks. "Not a dumb remark or an inappropriate comment? You won't even ask what I was expecting, the way I'm slacking off on the job?"

He responds by shaking his head and letting his gaze fall to his folded hands.

Ten seconds pass in silence, then ten more—and when, after half a minute, there is still no other answer from him, Yuki nods briefly, as if to say: *that's what I thought.* Then she turns her back on him and walks out the door.

CHAPTER 21

"So, today is the big day, huh?" the physiotherapist says, sporting his aggravating smile. "From now on, we won't be seeing each other every day anymore."

"Yeah, how will I ever survive?" Theodor replies.

"You'll be fine," the young sadist says—and as incredible as it sounds, he doesn't seem to get the sarcasm of Theodor's response. "How are you getting home, then?"

"My son and my daughter-in-law will give me a ride."

"Sounds nice."

"Yeah, some party that'll be."

The physiotherapist tilts his head slightly and looks at him.

"I think it would be good for you if you tried to be a bit more positive, Mr. Moody. You know, look at the bright side of things."

And I think it would be good for you to get a good, old-

fashioned kick in the butt. See how rosy everything looks to you then.

"That's good advice. I'll try."

Satisfied with that answer, the young man smiles at him once more. Then he stuffs the last things in his bag and swings it up on his shoulder.

"That's it then, Mr. Moody," he says, holding out his hand. "Take care of yourself—and don't forget to do the exercises I've given you, okay?"

Theodor reluctantly shakes his hand and responds with a humming sound lying somewhere in between *I will* and *are you still here?*

After seeing the physiotherapist's red torture bag disappear behind the door frame, Theodor leans back into the armchair. It has become his favorite spot now that he is no longer chained to the bed.

An hour later, he's still sitting there—head bent forward and nodding, eyelids heavy as lead weights—when three short knocks sound from the door.

"Hi, Dad. Can we come in?"

Theodor rubs his eyes and makes a little *yeah, go ahead* movement with his hand.

Kevin walks through the door and looks around the room, then takes a seat on a folding chair that the staff put in there for the occasion.

A second later, his wife goes through the exact same process, down to the tiniest detail. Even the disapproving expression at the sight of the folding chair

—*am I supposed to sit on that?*—is the same as Kevin had.

The businessman and his figurehead. So damned fussy. How the apple could fall that far from the tree is an eternal source of wonder for Theodor.

"It's gonna be great, huh, Theodor? To get out of here."

Basically, Theodor concurs. But he generally doesn't like to agree with his daughter-in-law, so he just grunts, saying:

"Well, it's not that bad here."

"No, and I bet it's been nice having dinner served every single day, right?" Kevin says.

"Oh, please," Theodor whispers, but apparently not sufficiently hushed because at once Kimberly's eyes widen in theatrical indignation.

"Excuse me. What did you say?"

"I said *oh, please*," Theodor repeats.

"And what is that supposed to mean?"

"The seat isn't even warm yet," Theodor elaborates, nodding toward Kevin's chair. "And already, we're on to the nursing home again."

"Care center," Kimberly corrects him in a *just so you know* tone of voice. "And who said anything about that?"

"I bet it's been nice having dinner served every single day, right?" Theodor parrots, glancing at his son.

"Actually, that's not what I meant," Kevin lies to his

father's face. "But now that the topic *is* on the table, then yeah, I do think we should talk about it."

With those words, Kevin looks innocently over to his wife as if to ask whether she too heard what an excellent idea he had just now.

And Kimberly, of course, nods and smiles just as enthusiastically as him. Then Kevin turns his attention back to Theodor.

"Where is the brochure that we gave you? Did you take a look at it?"

"I'm afraid the cleaning lady threw it out," Theodor says, nodding toward the trash can. He has to suppress a smile while doing so. "I think it had fallen to the floor."

"But did you look at it?"

"Oh yeah."

"And what do you think?"

Before Theodor can answer, he is interrupted by another knock at the door.

"Speak of the devil," he says, gesturing for the cleaning lady to come in.

Yuki takes a step into the room but then hesitates when realizing that both guests are leering at her.

"I ... can come back later," she says, but Theodor immediately shakes his head.

"Don't be silly! You just go ahead and do what you've got to do. You're not interrupting anything important."

"Well, I wouldn't say that," Kevin says. "To me, this seems pretty important."

"Yes, maybe it would be best if you could give us a couple of minutes," Kimberly adds, looking at the cleaning lady, but once again Theodor is on the defensive.

"Nonsense," he says. "There's no need to mess up her schedule just because you want to send me away. Besides, Yuki has been better at visiting me than my own family, so she's not going anywhere."

He hesitates a bit, and then a wry smile appears in the corners of his mouth.

"And just so you know. Where she's from, they take care of the elderly. They don't just hide them away."

Yuki hurries to turn her face away, under the pretext of reaching for a spray bottle of glass cleaner from the cart, but Theodor manages to catch the smile on her lips.

Good. It suggests that she has recovered from her breakdown yesterday. And that she's not mad at him anymore. At least not so much that his comment couldn't make her smile.

The two Ks, on the other hand, don't smile. Kevin looks exhausted, and Kimberly seems to be on the verge of a fit.

"No one is trying to hide anyone away!" she whispers between her clenched, Colgate-white teeth. "Kevin and I are just worried about you, and we think you would enjoy staying at a nursing home where there are qualified helpers and other residents your own age who—"

"Care center."

"Dad, don't."

"What?" Theodor says, dropping his hands to either side. "It's her own words. Not mine."

"Where there are other residents, your own age, that you can talk to," Kimberly repeats, obviously annoyed.

"I'm *not* going to a nursing home."

"With all due respect, Theodor," Kimberly says, "it's not your decision alone. And if you aren't capable of making the right choices for yourself, then ..."

She exchanges a look with her husband, and when Kevin subsequently clears his throat and leans forward, Theodor suddenly understands what's happening.

They're actually going to do it. They are going to force him.

"After what happened the last time we were here, we've talked a lot about it," Kevin says. "And we feel we'd be letting you down if we just pretended everything was fine and did nothing."

"I'm *not* going to a nursing home," Theodor repeats, although this time the words sound more like an animal's snarl than an actual sentence. "Did Chuck put you up to this? I told you he just wants to get back at me because—"

"The sheriff supports it, one hundred percent," Kimberly says. "But no, he hasn't talked us into anything."

Theodor looks inquiringly over at his son, who confirms his wife's words by slowly shaking his head.

A bitter indignation rises in Theodor, and he feels the urge to yell at Kevin, to disown him and tell him that he is no longer his son. That he can take his spotless suit and his spotless wife and go to hell.

And had his gaze not briefly wandered past Kevin and Kimberly's shoulders, to the cleaning cart behind them, he probably would have done just that.

But his gaze does drift over there and finds the dust cloth and the bottle of disinfectant hovering a few inches above the basket on its side.

Yuki has seen it too, and she reacts astonishingly fast. She grabs both from the air, placing them under her arm just before Kevin and Kimberly turn around to see what Theodor is staring at.

Yuki smiles politely with an assumed expression of confusion at them but says nothing.

That's the second time she has saved your old, wrinkly ass.

With this realization, an idea is born in Theodor's mind. Whether it's brilliant or outrageous, he isn't sure ... but it makes him pull his lips up in a smile. One that clearly concerns his son and daughter-in-law.

"But really, there's no need for us to keep talking about that nursing home," he says.

"And why is that?" Kevin sighs.

"Because I've already solved the problem," Theodor

explains. "I did as you suggested last time and found myself a helper."

"A helper?"

"Exactly. Someone who'll come to my house every day and lend a hand with the practical chores. That was what you suggested, wasn't it?"

Kevin's gaze turns to his wife, but there is no help to find this time. She looks just as dumbstruck as him.

"Um, yeah," he says. "I guess so. Who, um ... who is it?"

Theodor doesn't answer right away. Instead, he makes eye contact with Yuki—and holds it for as long as he needs to.

At first, she looks puzzled. Then the pieces start to fall in place for her, and she presses her lips together, making a strenuous swallowing motion.

On her cheek, a single tear moves downward in small jerks. She wipes it away, smiles gratefully at him ... and then she accepts the job offer with a small nod.

PART V
MERRY CHRISTMAS

"A church serves best those who look up when standing in it."

THINGS MARTHA USED TO SAY

CHAPTER 22

Snowflakes. Beautiful white crystals, thousands of them, dancing around in the garden to the ever-changing rhythm of the wind.

Yuki watches the snow waltz from inside the kitchen of Theodor's house, where she is putting away goods after the day's shopping trip.

That it should start snowing right now is almost *too* perfect. Today is the day when the Christmas holiday starts for her and Sammy.

To think that almost two months have passed since she started working for Theodor.

And to think that it has actually been a pleasure.

Sure, she's had to shake her head and bite her tongue from time to time, but on the whole, she has grown to like the old grump. And she's pretty sure the feeling is mutual ... although he probably wouldn't admit to it.

Sammy and Theodor have also developed a pretty close relationship. It came quite naturally given that Theodor's house is a lot closer to Sammy's school than the rehabilitation center was. This means that he has some time to spend every afternoon while he waits for her to finish up—and he spends that time with Theodor.

Typically, they do one of two things; they play chess, or they test Theodor's telekinetic skills. His *TK,* as Sammy calls it.

Today, the latter activity is on the schedule, and from her spot behind the kitchen window, Yuki can see that it's already well underway.

Sammy and Theodor, both wearing snowsuits, are standing down by the toolshed in the garden, next to a large woodpile. From it, Sammy picks up logs one by one and throws them into the air.

Theodor's task is obvious—catch without touching—and he does quite okay. A few slip past him and land on the snowy grass, but the majority he manages to slow down in the air and bring to the ground relatively calmly.

Yuki will probably never get used to the sight, but she has learned to accept it. Especially since the old man's abilities have lit a candle in her son's eyes that she can't remember having seen before.

Overall, Yuki's life has been pretty good lately. The home front has been calm, and she hasn't had to open the first-aid kit since ... well, not since the day with the bullies when Dean caught her with the bike out in the garage.

She had feared that he would give her a life lesson or two just over a week later when he discovered that Sammy's bike had been fixed. But the lie came to her surprisingly naturally—that she had found an instructional video on YouTube and fixed it herself—and he bought it. He wasn't exactly thrilled, which was expressed with a few condescending comments about women and tools, but at least he didn't use his fists that day.

That lie came easily. The one she's currently carrying around is harder. Not least because she has to share it with Sammy. She just can't see any other options, because if Dean learns that she lost her job at the rehabilitation center, he won't take it well. And if he, on top of that, found out that she's now working for a stranger she met at the center ... oh God, she can hardly finish that thought.

She winces when someone knocks on the kitchen window. She looks up and sees her son standing outside; eyes wide open, lips curved in a huge smile.

Mom, Mom, look! his mouth mimics as he points, directing her attention to Theodor in the garden.

The old man is standing with both hands spread to

the sides, palms up. Around him, snowflakes are still swirling around, forming random patterns in the air.

Except for those that are right above his hands. They hang statically in the air, drawing the outline of two large, inverted droplets. It almost looks like he's balancing two traffic cones made of semitransparent glass on his palms.

"Isn't it cool?" she hears her son's voice say. It's muffled by the glass of the kitchen window, but the enthusiasm passes through it with ease.

Oh, how she loves that boy. And how she hates having put him in a situation where he has to lie to his dad. Luckily, he didn't protest when she asked him to keep the layoff and her new job a secret for now. He just said okay, and she accepted it—without wondering if the boy might understand more of what was going on in their home than she had assumed.

Of course, he does. His mother happens to be sick for a few days every time he's been staying at Grandma and Grandpa's house. How gullible do you think he is?

"Yeah, Sammy," she replies as a chill, born from shame, runs down her spine. "It's very cool. Are you coming in soon? I only need to polish the mirror in the hallway, and then we're going home."

"Oh, okay," Sammy says. He is not entirely able to hide his disappointment, but at least he makes the attempt.

"Since it's the first day of the Christmas break, I thought we could ..."

Bake those cookies that you like would have been the rest of the sentence, but her son has already disappeared from the window.

Yuki sighs. Then she turns around and walks to the cupboard where Theodor keeps his cleaning products. From it, she grabs the cleaner spray for the mirror before continuing through the house until she gets to the hallway.

Theodor's house is exactly as one would expect. A modest but well-kept wooden house, built in a Cape Cod style with wood paneling on the walls, hinged shutters at the windows, and a garden nice enough to keep the neighbors in the suburban community from frowning too much.

Even the smell and sound in there is exactly what she had imagined. The air is warm and carries a faint note of tobacco, and all rooms are quiet except for the creaking of the wooden floors and the grandfather clock in the living room, whose heavy ticking reverberates throughout the house.

Not knowing better, one could be forgiven for thinking that the house stood empty. Still, it isn't hard for Yuki to imagine that there was life—and happiness—within these walls in the past.

It's the pictures that give it away. The photographs of

her. There is at least one in every room; Martha on a carousel, Martha on a sandy beach flying a kite with Theodor's son, Martha sitting on a folding chair in front of a camper with the Grand Canyon in the background, and—Yuki's favorite—Martha and Theodor sitting on a park bench holding hands.

So yes, even though Theodor clams up every time Yuki asks about his late wife, she feels no doubt: There was life here, and much of it disappeared along with Martha.

"Put that back!"

Yuki turns around and sees Theodor standing in the doorway to the living room. His eyes are focused on what she is holding in her hand—and he doesn't look pleased.

"Put it back," he repeats. "I pay you to clean the house. Not to put fingerprints all over my photos."

Yuki looks down at her fingers. They're gripping the corner of the frame, not touching the glass at all. But she recognizes, that's not what this is about.

"I'm sorry," she says and returns Martha to the small shelf above the mirror. "I was just wondering where it was taken."

"Next time, try looking with your eyes," Theodor mutters as he turns back toward the doorway. Before entering the living room, though, he hesitates for a moment and says, "Maiden Lake."

"What?"

"Maiden Lake. The photo was taken up at Maiden Lake. We ... I have a cabin up there where we used to go in the winter."

Yuki looks back at the picture. In its center, Martha is standing. She is wearing a red ski suit and a white beanie with tassels. The color of her cheeks—and the snow surrounding her—suggests that it's freezing, but her smile is warm. One of the warmest Yuki has ever seen. In the background, behind Martha, the snowy landscape is broken by the silvery surface of a large forest lake.

"It looks like a beautiful place."

"It is."

"Do you still go up there?"

"Not anymore."

For a moment, she can hear him holding his breath as if he's about to say something more, but either it's something she imagines, or he changes his mind. In any case, he disappears into the living room without saying anything else.

Yuki doesn't speak either. She simply swallows the lump in her throat and then resumes her work of polishing the mirror.

Five minutes later, she's done, which she lets her son know with a small nod as she enters the living room.

"Can't we stay a bit longer?" Sammy asks, nodding

toward the corner to her right, where there is a small table and two chairs. That's where they usually play chess. "I know I can beat him today."

"Now that would be a real Christmas miracle," Theodor grumbles, making the boy roll his eyes.

"Not today, sweetie. You'll have to save it for after the holidays."

Sammy tries his puppy eyes but quickly gives up when the desired result doesn't come.

"Well, then I wish you a wonderful Christmas holiday, Theodor," Yuki says. "Are you going to celebrate Christmas with your family?"

"Well, they did invite me, and they'll probably just come and pick me up if I stay home."

"Yeah, they probably will."

"What about you? I suppose you're gonna be eating rice and deep-fried chicken legs or something like that for Christmas, right?"

For a moment, she's on the defensive, ready to yell at him—for the umpteenth time—that she's not from China, but then she notices the faint hint of a smile in the corners of his mouth.

"You're a mean old man," she says, shaking her head. "You know that, right?"

"So I've been told," he replies, shaking her hand and then Sammy's. "And do take good care of this little troublemaker. We can't play chess if he has no fingers left after New Year's Eve."

"I'll take care of him," Yuki says, pulling her lips up in a smile.

Had she known what the Christmas holidays would bring for all three of them, that smile would probably never have seen the light of day.

CHAPTER 23

The turkey's skin is golden and crispy behind the glass in the oven door, the dinner table is almost set, the candles are lit, and in the background, Michael Bublé and Shania Twain dream of a white Christmas together.

In other words, it's Christmas Eve at the Rowley house, and all signs indicate that it will be a good one.

As per tradition, they have different roles: Yuki is in charge of the food, while Sammy decorates and sets the table. Dean chops the firewood and lights the fireplace. Oh, and usually he's also responsible for keeping Yuki's confidence in check by pointing out all the ways in which her Christmas dinner doesn't live up to the standard of his mother's ... but so far, he has refrained from doing so this year.

It's been going on for a long while now. His lenience. Part of her actually doesn't like it because it makes her nervous. Especially in the beginning, she had a nagging feeling that he was trying to lull her into a false sense of security so it would really hurt when he pulled the rug out from under her.

But the days went by, and now, two months later, her belly is still skin-colored. So maybe there is hope for better times.

"I'm done with the table, Mom!"

"That's good, sweetie. Will you give me a hand in here then?"

"Sure!"

A few seconds later, Sammy appears in the doorway, and Yuki can barely hold back a giggle. His eyes are so full of excitement that his pupils almost completely cover his brown irises. If it wasn't Christmas Eve, one might suspect that he was on drugs.

He's gonna be tossing and turning all night. You know that, right?

Yeah, she knows. Part of her has always thought that the American tradition of saving gifts until Christmas morning borders on child abuse. For the same reason, she has introduced a new tradition into their family, meaning that Sammy always gets one of his presents the night before. The so-called *swift gift*.

"What do you want me to do?"

"If you could grab the big cutting board and put it on the table over there. I'm gonna take the turkey out now."

Sammy nods and immediately sets about completing his task. Meanwhile, Yuki grabs the oven mitts, squats down, and opens the oven door.

"Careful," she hears Sammy whisper as she grabs the edge of the grate and starts pulling out the turkey.

It's heavy, a bit too heavy for her, actually, but she has no intention of asking Dean for help. She made that mistake once a few years ago, and it wasn't a great success. The turkey slipped a few inches on the grate, Dean scorched his hand ... and since it's of little use getting angry with a dead bird, he took it out on his wife instead.

So no, Yuki won't ask for help. She will get that turkey out of the oven and onto the cutting board all on her own.

As she slices it, she hears the door open in the hallway. With the sound comes a cold draft and then Dean's annoyed grunts as he edges his way into the living room with the wood basket. Both things cause her to twitch involuntarily.

"All I need to do now is heat the gravy," she says, glancing at Sammy. "Can you start carrying the rest of the food in?"

The boy nods, still with pupils dilated with Christmas excitement. Then he grabs a bowl and goes into the living room.

Yuki watches him as he does so. Her little boy. Her wonderful son, who by some miracle has inherited his father's good looks while avoiding to inherit his dark side.

Until now. These are two important words to remember. He has avoided it *until now*. But if he continues to live under the same roof, with Dean as his only male role model, his values will inevitably start to rub off. She already had a taste of that on Sammy's eighth birthday.

It doesn't matter, she tells herself. *In six months, we'll be out of here.*

"Is the gravy ready?"

This time, Yuki can't hold back the laughter, and when Sammy looks at her, partly confused, partly offended, it only gets worse.

"What's so funny?"

"You, my sweet boy," Yuki says, rubbing her eyes. "You're asking about the gravy, but what you really want to know is when we're done eating so it's time for the swift gift. Am I close?"

"Not at all," Sammy replies. "In fact, I'm looking forward to Christmas dinner, just so you know. I ... apprize it."

"You *apprize* it? What a fancy word. Well, that's good to hear. So maybe we don't even need the swift gift this year?"

Sammy's eyes transform into two tiny lines.

"Well, I wouldn't go *that* far," he says.

Yuki winks at him and points toward the plate on which the meat lies.

"Take that into the living room. I'll bring in the gravy in a minute."

When the minute has passed, Yuki follows him into the living room and puts the gravy boat on the table in front of Dean, who has already taken a seat.

"The table looks beautiful, Sammy," she says.

"Thanks, Mom. It was a bit hard when it's so big and we're just the three of us."

"Yeah, but there's nothing new about that, is there?" Dean says with a hint of irritation in his voice. "Grandma and Grandpa spend Christmas with Jimmy every two years. You know that, and there's nothing we can do about it."

Well, you could try mending the fence with Jimmy.

Yuki thinks this, but of course, she would never dream of saying it out loud. She knows there is a zero-tolerance policy toward mentioning Dean's older brother by name after their fallout four years ago. An event whose details Yuki has never dared to ask about.

"Do you want to say grace?" she asks, looking at Dean, but to her surprise, he just shakes his head.

Again, she feels a twinge of insecurity. It's not that Dean is religious, that would be a bold claim, but he is bound to traditions. He likes ... no, he *demands* a certain order and structure in things.

And he usually says grace at Christmas dinner.

"Are ... you sure?" she asks.

For a moment, Dean stares at her silently. Then he smiles and nods.

"Sammy has waited long enough," he says. "Don't you think?"

The smile on his lips looks fake. But the sparkle in his eyes seems genuine. In fact, it looks like Dean is burning with the same cocktail of excitement and impatience that she saw in her son's eyes earlier.

"Yeah, um ... yes, of course."

"Good," Dean says, nodding. "Now let's eat."

He reaches for the potatoes, shovels the three largest onto his plate, and then passes the bowl to Sammy.

"Eat, little man. We've got to put some muscle on you so you can knock the living daylights out of the next bullies who try anything."

He laughs at his own ingenuity and gives his son a nudge with his elbow, adding:

"Or Christmas lights!"

Yuki wants to say that it's an insensitive topic to bring up on Christmas Eve, but a look from Dean keeps her quiet.

Fortunately, Sammy doesn't seem to care about the comment. He just shrugs lightly and continues to scoop food onto his plate.

Forty-five minutes and two refills of the gravy boat later, they are still sitting at the table: Yuki and Sammy with empty plates, Dean with a plate housing a quarter of a potato which deftly slips aside every time the tip of his fork comes into contact with it.

In the end, however, he catches it—and when it's safely loaded into his mouth, he marks the end of the main course by letting go of his cutlery. It hits the plate with a clink that makes both Yuki and Sammy twitch.

"Oh, sorry," he says. But he doesn't mean it. It is a lie that his eyes are unable to convey believably.

Yuki feels her stomach contract again. Because she's getting more and more sure: He's hiding something. She just doesn't know what.

And whether it's something she should fear.

He looks like he's seen a stray dog riding a unicycle on the highway and can't wait until he gets the chance to tell someone, she thinks. *That's what he looks like.*

"Well," he says, looking at Sammy. "Don't you think it's time for you to get your swift gift?"

Sammy stares doubtfully at him and then at his mother.

"Shouldn't we eat the dessert first?"

"Yeah, that's ... what we usually do?"

Halfway through, the sentence becomes a question, and she glances over at Dean.

"I know, I know," he says, spreading his lips in a big smile. "I'm just excited about his gift this year. It's so good."

Yuki swallows. Her stomach isn't just restless anymore. It's aching.

Yes, Sammy's gift *is* good this year. Maybe the best one yet. A collectible figure, from a very limited edition, of his favorite superhero, Doctor Firestorm. She's spent weeks searching for it, and it felt like a minor miracle when it showed up at a secondhand market online.

But Dean doesn't know any of that. Because she's the one who takes care of the swift gift—and all of Sammy's other Christmas presents, for that matter. In fact, she's pretty sure he has no idea that Doctor Firestorm is his son's favorite.

She stares at Dean, who now places his hands on the edge of the table and pushes himself up.

Has she told him? No, she would remember that ... wouldn't she?

Dean lifts the potato bowl off the table and starts walking toward the kitchen, but when Yuki and Sammy reach for their plates to help, he stops and shakes his head.

"It can wait. Just stay here at the table. I'll find the gift."

Sammy glances, a little nervously, at Yuki, who shrugs her shoulders.

"Do you know where the gift is?" she asks, but Dean is already gone.

As relaxed and calm as possible—so as not to make Sammy nervous—she leans back in her chair and smiles at him.

He's not comfortable with Daddy's unexpected dismissal of the Christmas ritual either, and his eyes are asking her questions that she pretends not to see.

Now Dean returns, hands behind his back, huge smile on his lips.

"Are you excited?" he asks as he steps to the edge of the dining table.

For a split second, Sammy's eyes flicker over to Yuki again, but he catches himself in it and nods instead.

"You should be," Dean says, completely blind to the boy's discomfort. Or he doesn't care about it. "You'll never guess what it is."

Yuki realizes that Dean's gaze has shifted to her. That it was her he stared at as he said those last words.

Slowly, he takes his hands out from behind his back. He holds them out in front of himself, open and palms facing up. The same way one would hold them when carrying a platter of food.

But the object in his hands is not a platter. And it's not the gift Yuki bought for their son either.

"I think you took the wrong one," she says.

Dean looks down at the small box in his hands. Then he shakes his head and places the gift on the table in front of Sammy.

"Don't listen to your mother," he says. "It's the right one. She's just forgetful."

With slightly trembling fingers, Sammy starts to open the gift. However, he only manages to get the first piece of tape pulled off before his dad stops him by raising a hand.

But once again, it's Yuki he's staring at as he speaks.

"You've gotten so big now, so your mother and I think that you should be able to decide for yourself what you need. Right, Yuki?"

Even if she wanted to, Yuki couldn't give him an answer. Her throat is far too dry.

"That's why we've decided to give you money this year," Dean continues, his voice bright and cheerful ... but not in a good way.

Maybe Sammy's throat is also dried up. In any case, he is as silent as Yuki. He just stares at his father.

"Well, enough talk," Dean says. "Go ahead and open it."

Sammy hesitates for a moment, then presses a finger into the spot where the two ends of the wrapping meet.

Since he's sitting diagonally across from Yuki, the gift wrap still covers most of the box when he tilts it up, so Yuki can only see two of the letters printed on its front.

But those two letters—*HO*—are more than enough for her to identify the box and know what the rest of the word is. Because she has read it at least once a month for a very long time.

And the sight of it this time makes her chest tighten, as if two invisible hands have penetrated her chest, grabbed her lungs, and started squeezing.

HOTHEADS.

The matchbox from the basement—the one she thought was safely hidden beneath the loose tile under the washing machine—now lies in Sammy's small, innocent hands.

CHAPTER 24

"Be careful, it's slippery."

"I can see that it's slippery," Theodor snaps, grabbing the upper edge of the car door so he can lean on it as he gets out. "Even despite your wife's effort to blind me with that spectacle."

Kevin looks up at the facade of his house, which is decorated with fairy lights, reindeer, snowmen, and a glowing Santa Claus.

"Yeah, yeah," he says. "I'll be the first to admit that she goes a little overboard ... but she loves Christmas."

"A little overboard?" Theodor exclaims. "You practically live in a Coca-Cola commercial."

"Well, it's not *that* bad."

Theodor considers explaining why it *is* exactly *that* bad, but he concludes that if Kevin can stand here, mere yards from disco hell, and not be able to discern it himself, then it's probably not worth the effort. Ergo, Theodor merely shakes his head in resignation and walks up the tiled, and currently iced, path from the driveway to the front door.

That's another one of Kimberly's daft ideas that can make Theodor's blood boil. The path. Not only is it made with burgundy marble tiles as if it were a red carpet at a gala, it's also surrounded by two *Japanese gardens*, as she calls them.

What a load of crap! They're too lazy to keep a real garden, so what do they do? Unload a pile of gravel, rake it in circles, and call it a *Japanese garden*. Lord have mercy!

At least it's covered in a thin layer of snow now, so one can fantasize that there's a proper green lawn underneath.

At the end of the path, there is light behind the turquoise glass of the front door—and down at ground level, a dark, four-legged silhouette appears.

"That's still alive?" Theodor grumbles, and inside of himself he adds another *Lord have mercy*. "I didn't think the pocket-sized ones lived that long."

"Fifi? Yeah, she's fine. In fact, it's just the opposite. Small dogs generally live longer than large ones."

"Aha," Theodor replies, sighing. "Didn't know that."

Argument one: In his world, that little beast isn't a dog. A real dog can't fit in a handbag. A *rat* can fit in a handbag, yes. But not a dog.

Argument two: Despite its sparse intelligence, that little devil has no trouble remembering him. It knows exactly who he is, and it has never wavered in its attitude toward him.

In other words, the disapproval is mutual.

To the right of the door is the big, elongated kitchen window of Kevin and Kimberly's sterile designer house. Behind it, she stands, framed by a strange mixture of marble, stainless steel, and multicolored Christmas lights.

His daughter-in-law.

She's wearing a Santa hat. It's going to be a *long* night.

You should have insisted on driving yourself, Theodor thinks. *Then you could at least have decided when it ended.*

"Listen, I know it's not your favorite holiday," Kevin says as he stops in front of the door and puts his hand on its handle. "Especially not after ... well, you know. But I'm glad you agreed to celebrate Christmas Eve with us. And so is Kimberly."

As if she's heard her name mentioned, Kimberly raises her hand and waves at them from inside the kitchen. Theodor responds with a slight tilt of his hand and a half-hearted smile.

He also sends his son the same smile before replying, "I could hardly justify saying no, could I? It would be a waste of food if you had to share an entire turkey between two people."

Kevin sighs. Theodor pretends not to hear it.

Inside the hallway, Fifi welcomes her guest by barking, growling, and snapping at his pant legs. Amazing that such a puny instrument can make so much noise.

"That's enough, Fifi," Kevin says in a voice so devoid of authority that Theodor probably should be grateful that it, after all, is only a poodle—and not a human child—his son is responsible for raising. "I said enough, Fifi. You remember Grandpa, don't you? He won't bite."

There's always a first, Theodor thinks, staring at the dog with a look that he hopes gets that very message across to it.

Fifi couldn't care less about his hidden threats, but at least it has gotten tired of growling and barking now, so it turns around and disappears into the house. However, its substitute is only a split second away.

"Welcome, Theodor!" she says, waltzing across the floor, before stopping in front of him and planting a kiss on each of his cheeks, as if she thinks they are in some European capital where such a thing is okay. "And Merry Christmas!"

"Thanks."

For a moment, that short response triggers a blank expression on Kimberly's face. Then she shakes it off and smiles at him.

"Uh, I've got something for you. Stay here."

"Maybe we should let Dad come in and get warm

first, babe?" Kevin tries, but Kimberly just shakes her head.

"Relax. It's just a small thing, completely innocent. Besides, it's not really Christmas without one."

Kevin contorts his face, but he doesn't contradict her. Theodor says nothing either. For the sake of Christmas peace.

Kimberly claps her tiny hands and then runs into the house. When she returns, she is no longer able to clap. For her hands are holding Theodor's welcome gift.

"Isn't it cute?" she says, loosening her grip so the bottom half unfolds, revealing the monstrosity in its full splendor.

Theodor looks at his son, then at the Christmas sweater in his daughter-in-law's hands, then back at his son.

A cat in a baby carrier with a Santa hat and a milk beard, along with the words *I WISH YOU A 'MEOWY' CHRISTMAS* written below.

There are no words.

Bicycles, rocks, logs, hospital equipment. Theodor has been able to lift all of this, somewhat successfully, with his telekinetic powers. Now he considers if he would be able to lift a human being.

"Put it on," she says, holding it out to him. "It's for you."

With fingers he can no longer feel, he accepts the

sweater, mostly because he's so perplexed that he can't even get the words out to tell her where to stick it.

"Aren't you going to wear it?"

"It was a long drive with a lot of traffic," Kevin interjects as he grabs his wife's elbow and gently leads her into the house. "It's probably best we give him a moment to breathe. Right, Dad?"

Theodor responds with an absent nod and then lets his gaze fall back on the sweater in his hands. It lingers there for quite a while after Kimberly and Kevin disappear from sight. So do the four words that circle around in his head like a mantra.

When Hell freezes over.

Inside the living room, Kimberly has apparently also detonated a grenade full of Christmas knick-knacks. Every single architect-drawn corner houses at least one red, green, or luminous object.

"What would you like to drink?" Kevin asks.

Whatever is the strongest in your bar cabinet ... or in the medicine cabinet.

"I could go for a beer."

"I'll get it. You just kick back on the couch."

Theodor glances over at the couch where Fifi sits, watching him. Then he goes to the dining table instead, pulls out a chair, and takes a seat.

"It still feels weird, doesn't it?" Kevin says as he comes back from the kitchen with two cold Budweisers in his hand, one of which he gives to his father.

"What feels weird?"

"This," Kevin says, shrugging as he looks around the room. "Celebrating Christmas Eve without her."

Theodor nods in agreement, but only because he believes it to be the quickest way to end this conversation.

It doesn't work. Kevin continues, undeterred, down the dangerously icy streets of Memory Lane.

"She was a lot like Kimberly."

Theodor almost chokes on the mouthful of beer he's just taken, and he lets out a sputtering hiss.

"About Christmas, I mean," Kevin says. "Mom was crazy about it too."

"Mm, that she was."

A long pause. Then Kevin clears his throat.

"Yeah, it's sad to think about it, but I guess there's no point in getting hung up on the past. We just have to be happy about the time we got to spend with her."

"Mm."

Another long pause, which Kevin ends with a heavy sigh before lifting his beer as if he's saluting his mother's apparition. He has always been a drama queen. A pity he didn't spend the same energy expressing his love for her when she was alive.

Halfway expecting Kevin to start reciting poems or telling anecdotes about her through his childhood memories, Theodor peeks longingly out at the back patio, his roofless smoking shelter, but before he can say anything, Kimberly appears behind them.

"It's time to unbutton your belts and take a seat at the table, gentlemen. Christmas dinner is ready."

The food smells good and looks delicious. He has to give credit to their Christmas-fanatic chef for that. Even if the gravy is too thin. Real gravy should stick to the side of the potato when you fork it up. That's page one of the gravy manual.

"It's delicious, babe," Kevin says halfway through the first portion.

Kimberly smiles gratefully, then directs an expectant look at Theodor, who draws out the answer for as long as he can.

"Well, I guess it's not the worst Christmas meal I've had," he grumbles.

Kimberly exchanges a look with Kevin—*did you hear that?*—and then nods a thank you to her father-in-law.

"What about New Year's Eve?" Kevin asks.

"What about it?" Theodor replies.

"Are you going out, or are you staying at home?"

Theodor shovels a quarter of a potato into his mouth and chews it, very slowly, before answering.

"New Year's Eve is at home on Rue Lane. It's been that way every year since we bought the house. Why should that suddenly change?"

"Oh, I don't know," Kevin says, shrugging. "I just thought it might be nice for you to get out, now that ..."

"Yeah?"

"Now ... that you're on your own."

Theodor's eyes answer for him.

"What Kevin is trying to say is that you're welcome to celebrate the New Year at our house if you'd like some company," Kimberly explains. "I'm making miso-glazed Chilean sea bass with honey-roasted rainbow carrots in burrata."

Yes, of course, you are.

"Thanks, but I prefer to stay at home."

"Are you sure? We don't mind."

Theodor takes one, two, three deep breaths. Then he repeats his rejection of the offer—this time in the form of a slight shake of the head—and pushes his chair out from the table.

"You'll have to excuse me," he says. "The food is lying pretty heavily in my stomach, and I think I need to get some fresh air before round two."

"Some tar-filled air, you mean," Kevin says.

The fourth breath becomes extra long and deep. So deep that it almost hurts Theodor's chest to keep the air in.

But he does. He waits to let it out until he's turned his back on them—and he resists the temptation to let a few swear words out along with it.

CHAPTER 25

"H-how?"

That's the only word Yuki is able to squeeze out, and afterward, she's not even sure she's actually said it out loud, because everything feels unreal. Like a fever dream.

"Oh, yeah," Dean says, pretending to give himself a smack on his forehead. "I forgot to tell you."

His hand moves toward hers, but she pulls it away before he can touch it. His gaze, however, she can't pull away from. It feels like acid on her skin.

"We had water damage," he continues. "Nothing too serious, just a leaky pipe ... but it caused a flood in the basement. And to get to the pipe, I had to move the washing machine."

Don't do it! Yuki says to herself as she feels a familiar

burn behind her eyeballs. *Don't cry! Don't give him that pleasure!*

"A hundred dollars!" Sammy announces next to her, pulling the contents, two fifty-dollar bills, out of the HOTHEADS matchbox. "Thanks, Dad. Thanks, Mom."

He spontaneously gets up, walks over to Yuki, wraps his arms around her—and then the battle is lost. Ice-cold tears begin to roll down her cheeks, blurring her vision.

She hugs him back and holds him tight, hoping that by doing so she can drag the moment out until her tears have dried up, but the boy only gives her a handful of seconds before he starts pulling away.

"What's wrong, Mom?"

"Mom was just moved, seeing how much you liked the gift," Dean says.

"Is that why, Mom?"

Yuki sniffles and pulls in a few mouthfuls of air. Then she forces a smile and nods at him.

Sammy's hand affectionately strokes her shoulder. Then he turns around and walks over to Dean.

"Thanks for the gift, Dad. I don't think I've ever had that much money at once before."

"You're welcome, Sammy," Dean says, leaning forward so he can give the boy's shoulder a squeeze. And so he can look at Yuki over Sammy's head as he continues, "We know it's a lot of money, Sammy, but you're a big boy now. In fact, I was considering giving you a lot more

—all that could fit in the box—but Mom and Dad also need money for rent and food, right?"

Sammy responds with an *oh, you're so silly* shake of the head, then walks back toward his seat. However, he only manages to take two steps before Dean taps him on the shoulder.

"Listen, would you mind cleaning up the rest? Your mom needs a break, and I need to kick back."

His peculiar choice of words may be a coincidence, but his eyes suggest that it isn't.

Sammy nods, grabs a few bowls, and then disappears into the kitchen. Now there are only the two of them left. Yuki and her husband.

For a while, none of them say anything. He sits and stares at her, with the reflection of the candle flame dancing in his night-dark pupils, and she uses all her strength to maintain eye contact. On not giving him the victory it would be if she looked away.

"Nothing?" he suddenly asks. "Not even an *oh, Dean, I can explain*?"

As he speaks, he lets his hands fall out to the sides and throws his voice up into a shrill falsetto to imitate her—and during this theatrical performance, Yuki has an epiphany:

Dean *hates* her. He *loathes* her. It's not just in those situations where a misstep on her part triggers his anger, that she's a dull-witted, useless bitch in his eyes. It's every minute of every day.

But why didn't he throw her out a long time ago, then? Because she's his—and Dean Rowley doesn't share his toys. Whether he himself wants to play with them or not.

"I asked you a question," he says.

"I heard you."

"And?"

"It makes no difference what I say, does it?"

He bites his lower lip and looks down at his hand, which he clenches—undoubtedly for her viewing pleasure—so it forms a fist. Then he shakes his head slowly.

From the kitchen, there is a rattle of plates, and a new wave of panic washes over Yuki.

"It's Christmas Eve, Dean. Can't we—"

He shakes his head again, even slower.

"In a way, it's my own fault," he says. "I see that now. I've been too trusting, given you way too long a leash. The both of you."

"What are you *saying*?" Yuki whispers, once more glancing nervously toward the kitchen. "Sammy has nothing to do with this. He is—"

Dean interrupts her by letting out a hiss and baring his teeth, making him look like a wild animal.

"Maybe not with the matchbox," he snarls. "But your other little secret. Sammy must know about that."

"I-I don't know what you're talking about."

"Your job. That you were fired."

She opens her mouth, but the question she wants to

ask is stuck in her throat, and the only thing coming out is a hoarse sigh.

"I was a bit confused when I found your little ... stash," Dean explains. "So, I called your workplace and had a chat with your boss. Ms. McKinney? Was that her name?"

Yuki remains silent, but it doesn't matter. Dean doesn't wait for an answer. He just continues his story.

"And as you can probably imagine, my confusion didn't exactly lessen when she told me that you don't work there anymore."

He brings his clenched hand up to his temple and spreads his fingers in dramatic slow motion, his mouth mimicking the sound of an explosion.

"She probably thought I was a bit rude," he continues, when the last, resounding echo of the explosion has faded. "In any case, she clammed up when I asked if she knew where you got your money from now. To be honest, I don't think she believed I was your husband. The nerve, huh?"

Whether Dean expects her to nod or in other ways agree with that interpretation, Yuki can't quite decide. She chooses to stay quiet, hoping it won't anger him further.

"I thought about stopping by to have a serious talk with her. See if she'd be more compliant face to face ... but then it hit me: Why on earth would I do that when I can just ask you?"

Out of the corner of her eye, Yuki sees the fingers of her hand twitching involuntarily, and she instinctively moves it from the edge of the table onto her thigh. No need to openly display how terrified she is.

"I promise I'll tell you everything, but I think we should ask your parents if Sammy can stay with them tonight ... or at least wait to talk until he's in bed."

"They always stay until past midnight when they spend Christmas over at Jimmy's, so it's gonna be way too late. Besides, Sammy isn't going anywhere. Not this time."

The words hit Yuki like a fist in the solar plexus, forcing out a gasp.

"If he's big enough to lie to me, he's big enough to have a serious talk about it afterward."

"No, Dean. Oh God, please no. He's just a kid."

"Where does the money come from, Yuki? The McKinney moron said you were laid off two months ago, but you're gone every day and there's still money going into the account. So, where the hell does it come from? Are you turning tricks? Is that it?"

"I ... what? No!"

"Nah, I guess no one would want to pay to ruffle up someone like you."

It's almost a gift. He can spit out something so condescending, so *vicious*, and still make it sound like he's just citing a commonly known fact. *The moon orbits the Earth, the grass is green, and no one on this planet would dream of jumping in the hay with my raggedy dishcloth of a wife. Let alone pay for it.*

"But then where?" he whispers. "Where does the damn money come from?"

She opens her mouth, not knowing what to say. Not that it makes any difference, because at that instant, Sammy appears on the edge of her field of vision.

The boy continues past her to the other side of the table, where he picks up Dean's dirty plate. Meanwhile, Yuki lets her gaze drift down to her own plate—and to the knife lying on top of it, glistening temptingly in the glow of the candle.

He'll kill you if he sees you.

A fair point—and had Dean not threatened to punish Sammy, she would undoubtedly have conformed to that argument.

But he did. He crossed the invisible line that has always been there. He brought Sammy into the game.

With that thought gnawing at the back of her mind, Yuki waits for the right moment, and when Sammy leans in over Dean to take the fork that's still on the table, her hand shoots out like a cobra, grabs the knife, and hides it away on the chair seat under her left thigh.

CHAPTER 26

In fact, something has been put out for the purpose. A multicolored porcelain bowl, probably made by some famous designer that Theodor has never heard of.

But it's a bowl, not an ashtray, and that means that the wind pulls up the ashes and throws them back at him every time he knocks the cigarette against the edge of it. It is an impossible battle to win. Like Goofy trying to load a stubborn piano onto a truck in the old cartoons. It always comes back.

For forty years, Theodor has smoked. For seven years, Kevin and Kimberly have lived here, chasing him out on the back patio to smoke ... and not once have they provided a real ashtray with a lid.

Inadvertently? Not a chance. Therefore, Theodor also feels no remorse about ending his smoking ritual by extinguishing the cigarette against the marble tiles, leaving a small, gray-black stripe of ash.

At the bottom of the outer wall to his left is a basement window. Behind it, Theodor can make out a part of a wine rack and the handlebars of a bike.

The sight of the latter makes him wonder what Sammy and Yuki are doing right now. It has to be more entertaining than this.

To think that he would actually prefer to celebrate Christmas with his cleaning lady rather than his own family.

A sliding sound makes him twitch. He turns around and sees Kevin standing at the patio door.

"Are you ready?"

"Yeah, I'm coming."

Inside the living room, Kimberly has been busy. All the dishes and bowls on the dining table have been refilled, and the whole room is enveloped in a heavy, humid heat that smells of turkey.

"If you hand me your plate, I can give you another round while I'm standing," Kimberly says.

She smiles, but her voice seems a bit cold. The most likely reason is that he has been discussed while he was out smoking. But hell, they can complain about him all they want. Had he had a fellow sufferer out on the patio, the hosts would also have been thoroughly talked about, that's for sure.

"Only a little bit, please," he says, handing her his plate. "I need room for the rice pudding."

Kimberly smiles again, more genuinely this time.

"I've tried something new this year," she says.

"What does that mean?" Theodor asks, even though he has a pretty good guess. And he is not at all surprised when the answer comes.

"You'll probably think I'm crazy," she says. "But I promise you that you won't know the difference."

She pauses dramatically, her eyes sparkling so much that you'd think she's about to tell him he's going to be a grandpa or something.

"It *is* rice pudding," she says. "Just in a healthier version so we don't have to diet all of January. It's made with Greek yogurt, cottage cheese, and vanilla. No cream at all."

A rusty, metallic taste hits Theodor's tongue, and he realizes that he has bitten himself on the inside of his lower lip.

"So, it's a rice pudding ... without rice?" he moans.

Kimberly's smile widens as if that were a compliment.

"It sounds too good to be true, I know. But the cottage cheese gives the texture, and you can't taste the difference at all. It's just like the one Martha used to ..."

She realizes she's crossed the border into a minefield, and her gaze flickers nervously over to Kevin as if she wants to ask him if he thinks Theodor heard.

Theodor did—and if Kimberly and Kevin turned around and looked, his inner reaction would be visible on the shelf above the television, where a turquoise vase rises in the air, shaking unsteadily.

On the couch, Fifi begins to growl, looking vigilantly from side to side.

Theodor tries to ignore it. Getting the vase to land again without tipping it over is hard enough. He doesn't need the watchful eyes of that little overachieving rat as an additional stress factor.

"What's the matter, Fifi?"

The little beast answers its owner by jumping off the couch and looking up at the floating vase while growling extra loudly.

Theodor, now with his heart racing in his chest, squints his eyes and forces every cell in his body to work together with one common goal—to get the vase back down before Kevin and Kimberly follow the dog's gaze upward.

The vase lands at the very last second, and although it tilts a few times from side to side before finding its balance, none of them seem to notice anything suspicious.

Kevin gives his dog a disapproving look—to which Theodor adds a mocking smile. One that says: *You thought you had me, huh?*

"I just don't know what's gotten into her today," Kimberly says as the poodle creeps back onto the couch.

"She could probably feel the atmosphere getting a little tense," Kevin says.

Kimberly adopts a troubled expression and nods.

"Yes, I'm sorry about that, Theodor," she says. "It just flew out of me."

"What flew out of you?"

"Well, um ... her name."

Theodor doesn't answer. He just continues staring at her as if he doesn't understand what she means. He does, of course, but Kimberly opened the box herself, so now she'll have to bite the bullet and say the name out loud again.

"Martha," she says. "I should have known that it would ... affect you to hear her name. Especially around Christmas."

Theodor has his answer ready on the tip of his tongue, but before he gets to throw it at her, Kevin seizes the opportunity to make things worse.

"Sometimes it's the littlest things," he says, wistfully looking out the window. "A song on the radio or a woman in the supermarket who has the same jacket as her, and swish—it's like you've been thrown back in time, and it's only been a day since she passed away."

In Theodor's defense, he does try. He does his best to suppress his indignation and keep his lips sealed.

But.

"You egocentric little brat," he growls. "Who the hell do you think you are?"

For a moment, Kevin stiffens, looking like he's been frozen in time. Then he blinks his eyes and tilts his head, as people do when an insect flies close to their face. Or when they have been deeply shocked.

"W-what did you say?"

"You heard me," Theodor says. "I called you an egocentric little brat. Because that's what you are."

"You can't talk to him like that," Kimberly begins, but for Theodor, at this moment, she could just as easily be the tiny, invisible insect that made Kevin blink.

"You talk about your mother's death as if it made your world collapse," he continues, his voice sounding so guttural and snarling that he can hardly recognize it as his own. "As if she were an angel. But where were you when she got sick, huh? Where were you when bloodstains started appearing on her sleeve every time she coughed? And where were you when she was restricted, first to a wheelchair, then to a bed?"

"We visited her!"

Theodor lets out an offended sniffle and shakes his head.

"Ha! You brought her flowers, yes!"

"And what's wrong with that?"

"She didn't need flowers! She needed care. She needed to be held, to be stroked over her hair, to be fed and bathed, to be ..."

The words become thicker, bulkier, and he finds it harder and harder to get them out through his throat.

And the longer they're stuck in there, the more his powerlessness and sadness take over from the anger.

"She needed more than me," he finally whispers. "Not someone who tossed a bouquet in the door when passing or sat with half an eye on his wristwatch during the entire visit because there was an important meeting later. She needed her whole *family*. Her *son*."

"Dad, I ..."

Nothing more than those two words comes out of Kevin's mouth. Not that it matters. The fight is over. Theodor understands that. He also knows that there is no winner. Because Martha is gone and there are no victories left to be had.

The silence that follows in the wake of the argument is long and awkward. All three of them study the gold patterns on the edges of Kimberly's Christmas plates more thoroughly than they've ever been studied before.

Even when the silence becomes too much for his daughter-in-law, and she asks if they want more before she brings in the dessert, neither Theodor nor Kevin looks up. They simply respond by shaking their heads slightly.

CHAPTER 27

"I'm still waiting for that explanation," Dean whispers through the clenched teeth of his predatory smile. "Where does the money come from?"

Yuki is still sitting across from him on the other side of the dining table, but it feels like she's sitting on the floor in the corner with him towering above her.

No escape. If she tells the truth, Dean's extreme jealousy will undoubtedly drive him to seek out Theodor. In the best case, just to beat him up. If she tells a lie, she might be able to buy some time, but not much. After all, Dean is a cop, and she has no doubt that he will use all his resources to find out if she's bullshitting him.

Cholera or the plague. That's what she has to choose from. And the clock's running out because she can hear that Sammy is done rinsing the plates in the kitchen and has started loading the dishwasher.

She spins a mental wheel of fortune and chooses the golden middle ground. A half-truth.

"I was offered a job as a helper for one of the patients from the rehabilitation center."

She lets the words hang in the air between them as she studies the reaction on Dean's face. He still looks sinister, but there's a hint of something else. It looks like surprise. Maybe it's because he was expecting a lie but then was told by his police instincts that she's telling the truth.

"A kind old lady," Yuki continues. "Her family wanted to put her in a nursing home, but she wanted to stay in her house. So when she heard that I was being laid off, she offered that we could help each other. I could get a new job and she could keep her home."

"I see," Dean says as he reaches for his wine glass and then begins to spin it aimlessly in his hand. "That was quite the lucky coincidence, huh?"

Round and round, he spins it while the reflections of the candle flames dance in the glass, making it look like a miniature version of a fairground carousel.

"And why haven't you told me about this ...?"

"Mrs. Moody," Yuki replies, immediately realizing that she's jumped right into his first trap with both legs. He caught her in an incomplete lie and made her expand on it, without giving her the chance to think. All by turning a stupid wine glass so that her attention was diverted.

Nicely done, Yuki. Now he has a last name.

"I didn't tell you about the new job because I was afraid of how you would react," she says, hoping that another truth will confuse his instincts again and make the lie more convincing. "I was ... embarrassed and nervous that you'd get angry."

"You underestimate me," Dean says. "You know I've always thought that ridiculous cleaning job was a waste of time when I earn enough for you to stay home. So, you losing that wouldn't have made me angry at all."

"Mm," Yuki replies, feeling a chill run over her spine at the thought of becoming a housewife. Becoming his little trophy wife-slash-slave. "I know."

Moreover, one would have to look long and hard to find a bigger lie. Because Dean *would* have gotten angry. He would have asked her how stupid you have to be to get fired from a *cleaning job*. And then he would have pummeled her senseless. But since pointing out that detail would be like trying to put out a campfire with a bucket of lighter fluid, Yuki keeps her mouth shut.

"Being lied to by one's wife and son, on the other hand," Dean continues. "Now, that's something else. You could get a little angry about that."

Yuki says nothing, but her fingers instinctively find their way down to the knife she has hidden on the seat under her left thigh.

"But hey," Dean says, shrugging. "I shouldn't jump to

conclusions. Who knows? You could be telling the truth. Luckily, we can easily find out."

He turns around on his chair so he's facing the doorway to the kitchen.

"Sammy! Come in here for a sec, would you?"

The boy appears in the doorway and stays there for a moment, looking back and forth between his parents.

"What is it?"

"Just a little game," Dean says, gesturing for him to come closer. "Mom has got a new job. You know that, right?"

Sammy exchanges an uneasy look with Yuki. Then he nods hesitantly.

"Of course, you know," Dean says. "The two of you ride together every day, so you must have been there. Ergo, you must know the person Mom works for now, right?"

Sammy bites his lip, and the confusion on his face turns to anxiousness. However, he doesn't have time to say anything before Dean stops him with a raised hand.

"Don't say it yet!" he says. "It'll ruin the game."

"Dean ..." Yuki tries, but she is also stopped by him. Not with a raised hand, but with an icy look, promising a world of suffering if she doesn't put a sock in it.

"Good," Dean says. "The game goes like this: I count to three, and then you two say the name of Mom's new boss, at the same time, loud and clear. Understood?"

"Mom?" Sammy stammers, but it's his dad who

answers, sharply and concisely, by pounding his fist on the table and repeating the last word.

"UNDERSTOOD?"

Sammy winces, and so does Yuki. In fact, she almost drops the knife that she has pulled out from under her thigh and is now holding in a trembling hand beneath the edge of the table.

Its metal feels freezing against her skin. As if it were a foreign object her body tries to reject. Part of her also wants to let it go. To give up and just surrender, as she has done countless times before.

But she is no longer the only one who has seen the monster's true face. This time Dean has pulled off his mask with Sammy in the room.

And she has to draw the line there.

"Are you ready?" Dean asks, and without waiting for an answer, he starts counting: "One ..."

"Please, Dean. I'm begging you."

"Two ..."

"Dean, for God's sake. You're scaring Sammy."

"Three!"

She stubbornly closes her mouth and remains silent.

When he sees her doing it, Sammy copies her and does the same. But by then it is too late. That one, fateful word has already left his mouth.

Now it hangs there between them, in an air so charged with electricity that you can almost hear it humming and crackling.

"Theodor?" Dean repeats, looking at his wife so intensely that it feels like he's trying to test the old saying and spot her soul behind her eyes. "Interesting name for an old lady."

"Sammy, go to your room," Yuki says in a voice she can barely control.

"He's not going anywhere," the monster snarls on the other side of the table.

"Sammy, go to your room!" Yuki repeats, not shifting her gaze from Dean. "And lock the door."

"Stop it," Sammy orders, but his voice is little more than a mushy whisper. "Both of you. Stop it."

"Do you see?" Dean asks, looking at her as he points toward the boy. "Do you see what you've done to him? What a girl he's become? That's because of *you*. All your fussing and coddling!"

Sammy's crying now, and Dean gives an extra flick in the air with his outstretched hand as if to say: *Well, there you go. Now the little girl is crying.*

"He's become a whiny sissy because we've been too soft," he continues, putting his hands on the edge of the table and pushing himself up. "But I'll fix that!"

"NO!" Yuki screams, and before she knows it, she's on her feet, knife in hand, its shivering blade aimed at Dean as she moves in between him and Sammy. "Don't you touch him!"

Dean focuses his gaze on the knife and, afterward, on her face. Then he pulls his lips up in the most condescending smile Yuki has ever seen. If he's the slightest bit intimidated by her improvised weapon, he hides it incredibly well.

"I'll give you one chance to do a U-turn," he hisses. "Throw the knife on the floor and beg for forgiveness. Then we'll pretend that this bright idea never entered your little head."

"Stay where you are," Yuki replies. She tries to sound tough but fails. More than anything, the words come out sounding like a series of pathetic moans.

Without shifting her gaze from Dean's face, she reaches her arm back and gropes blindly in the air until she finds Sammy's shoulder. Once she has it, she gently pushes him toward the kitchen door.

He is terrified. She can feel him shaking underneath her fingers. It pains her, but she has to push it aside. She doesn't have time to deal with either his or her own panic. Right now, they just need to get out. Out of the house and as far away from Dean as—

She registers the movement as Dean's hand, without warning, shoots over to the table, but he is incredibly fast, and before she can react, he has grabbed the edge of the tablecloth and pulled it off. It now flies toward her, covering her field of vision with Christmas trees, snowmen, stars, and red hearts.

She screams, swinging the knife frantically from side to side in front of her. Two small cuts appear in the fabric where the knife hits, but the tablecloth doesn't lose speed. It falls on her, enveloping her in claustrophobic darkness.

A second later, she feels Dean's strong arms close around her torso. He squeezes hard and shakes her from side to side until she loses both the knife and her footing.

What her face collides with when he lets go and lets her fall helplessly to the ground, she has no idea, but it must be one of the larger pieces of furniture, maybe the cabinet because it doesn't budge an inch. Her nose, on the other hand, does. At least that's how it feels.

She pushes, pulls, and punches the tablecloth to break free from its suffocating embrace.

Somewhere outside the darkness of the acrylic straitjacket, she hears Sammy sobbing as he begs his father to stop. She tries to join in, tries to yell for Dean to stop, but nothing comes out of her mouth. Not even air.

Run, Sammy! she thinks as if hoping to reach him through a telepathic ability she had no idea she had. *Get out of here!*

But when she finally fights her way out of the tablecloth and looks out into the living room through a filter of smudged colors and silvery, flickering spots, she sees that Sammy hasn't gotten away.

He tries, yes, but Dean's grip on the boy's arm is far too strong, and Sammy doesn't stand a chance. He is dragged around effortlessly by his father as if he were a jointless rag doll.

Steeped in panic and desperation, Yuki pulls herself across the floor to grab the knife that has ended up under the dining table.

"Just give it up already, Yuki," Dean grumbles, but she continues unabashedly. She has obeyed his orders for the last time, and she's not going to stop until that knife is lodged in his throat.

That's the last thought Yuki has before Dean's foot hits her at full strength just below the ribs on her right side, pushing every last bit of air out of her.

After that, her whole world sinks into a deep, pitch-black sea.

PART VI
MAIDEN LAKE

"The older the fiddle,
the sweeter the tune."

> Things Martha used to say

CHAPTER 28

His face is blurred. Wavering, as if she's lying at the bottom of a murky swimming pool, observing him through a water surface in motion. A pale, rippling mask that alternately sharpens and liquifies.

"Mom?" he says, and the sound of his voice calms the water, revealing more details of his face.

Sammy. It's Sammy's face.

"Mom, you need to wake up! Wake up, Mom!"

He grabs her shoulders and shakes them. She can tell from his face that he strains himself, yet she can barely feel his touch.

"What ... happened?" she squeezes out through her bone-dry throat, but hardly have the words crossed her lips before the answer comes to her on its own. Through a series of images flickering past her inner gaze:

The HOTHEADS matchbox surrounded by torn

wrapping paper. Dean's condescending smile. The knife on the table. Dean's condescending smile. Same knife, now in her trembling hand. Dean's condescending smile.

"I'll give you one chance to do a U-turn. Throw the knife on the floor and beg for forgiveness. Then we'll pretend that this bright idea never entered your little head."

"Where is he?" she moans as she pushes herself up into a sitting position. "Sammy, where's Dad?"

When there is no answer, she looks at the boy—and realizes that he is, understandably, on the verge of a breakdown. His lips quiver, his eyes are wet and red.

She ignores the pain in her stomach, grabs Sammy, and pulls him in close—and then his tears can't be held back anymore. He buries his face in her shoulder and sobs.

"I-I didn't know if you would wake up again," she hears him say, and her heart feels like it's being ripped out of her chest. "I'm so sorry, Mom."

"God, no, Sammy. It's not your fault. None of this is your fault."

"But Dad got angry about what I said."

"No, Sammy," she says, gently rocking him back and forth like she did when he was little. "What you said made no difference. He was already angry."

The boy doesn't answer. He just shakes a bit more—she hopes it's out of relief—and then he slowly calms down.

Meanwhile, Yuki blinks a few times to remove the worst spots from her field of vision and then looks around the semi-dark room. The smell—concrete, washing powder, and damp wood—has already revealed to her where they are, so it doesn't surprise her that the first thing she spots is the washing machine by the back wall. The hiding place that failed her and caused all of this.

At some point, while she was unconscious, Dean dragged her down to the basement. His motive? She can only speculate, but probably nothing good.

She waits as long as she dares, then loosens her grip on Sammy and repeats her original question.

"I need to know where Dad went, sweetie. Do you know where he is?"

"He's gone," the boy mutters. "He ... he locked the door, Mom. We can't get out."

Yuki looks up, locates the basement stairs and the door at the end of it. Since it's the only door down here, it must be the one Sammy is talking about, but ... how can it be locked?

It can't. The lock is on the inside.

Hardly has she finished this thought before the most obvious explanation hits her. An explanation she doesn't want to believe.

"Help me up, Sammy," she moans, putting her arm over his shoulders and neck.

The boy stares at her uncertainly for a moment. Then he puts his arm around her back and pulls her up.

Together they struggle their way across the cold concrete floor toward the stairs. Once they're there, she grabs the railing—a worn-down board that wiggles if you don't know where to grab it—and uses it to stay upright.

The door is also old and worn. If she's lucky, that's the explanation; that it's damp and therefore sticks, so it's difficult for Sammy to open.

A mixture of disappointment and a fear she doesn't quite understand hits her as she turns the handle and pushes.

Her premonition held true. The door doesn't stick. It is fixed in place, not budging an inch. Dean has blocked it, probably with some heavy piece of furniture. Maybe he's even taken the time to nail it shut with some of the boards from the garage.

"What's wrong with him, Mom?" she hears Sammy say behind her. "Why is Dad acting like this?"

His voice is frail, full of fear, confusion, and worry. Full of the same emotions that are swirling around inside of her.

"Your dad is not well, Sammy," she says because that's the only explanation she can give right now—and because it's partly true. "And we've got to get out of here before he returns. Do you have any idea where he went?"

Sammy's face contracts in shame, and his gaze falls to the ground.

"H-he said he'd push you down the stairs if I lied to him. I couldn't ..."

"Lied about what, Sammy? What did he want you to say?"

Sammy's hands start to shake. Soon after, his shoulders follow. On his cheeks, tears sparkle in the light of the fluorescent lamps above them.

"Sammy?" Yuki repeats, placing her hand on his shoulder. "What did he want you to say?"

"Mr. Moody," Sammy murmurs. "H-he wanted to know where Mr. Moody lives."

"And you told him?"

"I had no choice, Mom. He said he ..."

The last words drown in the boy's tears, but that's okay. Yuki doesn't need to hear them. She knows what Dean is capable of. How *persuasive* he can be when he shows his true colors.

"It's okay, Sammy," she says, tightening her grip on his shoulder. "You hear me? It's okay. You couldn't have done anything else. Okay?"

She catches his gaze, maintains eye contact, and waits until he's given her a nod. Then she turns around and begins to move back down the stairs.

"What are you going to do?"

"We need to get out of here so we can warn Theodor."

In the southwest corner of the basement is an old plastic barrel which Dean, at some point, turned into a storage unit for old junk. Within this category falls, among other things, the handful of metal poles that were left after he replaced the fence around the herb patch in the garden.

It's one of those poles that Yuki reaches for and then carries with her to the opposite side of the basement.

Its surface is brown with rust, but the metal of the pole is still strong enough for what she has in mind. At least that's what she hopes.

A dry, crunching sound fills the room as she hammers one end of the pole against the wooden frame of the small window.

"Can't we just open it?" Sammy asks.

Yuki shakes her head and points to a hinge on the left side of the window.

"It's just for airing out, so it only opens a little bit. We'll have to break the hinges off completely if we want to get it open."

"What if we break the glass?"

"Too dangerous. The window is far too small for us to squeeze through without cutting ourselves on the shards."

Another blow—using all her strength—and the only result is a scratch, two or three inches long, at the outer edge. And it feels like she's done significantly more damage to her ribs than to the window frame.

With the state you're in, this is going to take you an hour. Minimum. You know that, right?

Panic stirs, threatening to take control of her body, and she has to concentrate to prevent it from happening.

"When did Dad leave?" she asks. "How long has it been?"

"I don't know," Sammy shrugs. "Half an hour, maybe."

Yuki nods. It isn't quite the answer she was hoping for, but at least it gives her an approximate deadline. Because even if the boy's sense of time is a little skewed, it should be a while before Dean's Ford Raptor reappears in the driveway.

This leaves the question of how to best use her remaining energy reserves before then.

She looks up at the willful window, then at the basement stairs, and finally down at the pole in her hand. Then she grabs Sammy's hand and pulls him with her.

CHAPTER 29

Silence is an interesting—albeit sometimes contradictory—phenomenon. In its essence, silence means that everything is quiet. No sounds to hear, in other words. Yet, authors, journalists, and other navel-gazing wordsmiths often choose to spice things up with the addition of adjectives like *deep* and *complete*.

But where exactly lies the difference between silence and *absolute* silence? Nowhere, if you ask Theodor. But then again; Who is he to speculate on such long-haired academic issues? After all, he exchanged the school bench for the seat of one of *Gleamsdale Bugle's* newspaper distribution bikes as soon as the opportunity presented itself.

However, one thing is certain: if the keyboard boxers are right and absolute silence exists, the same conjugation must also be applicable to awkward silence. If so, that's what's prevailing in the car right now.

Absolute awkward silence.

He casts a discreet glance to the left, where Kevin sits with his hands on the steering wheel and his eyes almost manically fixated on the road ahead.

It's a bit slippery outside, but that's not why he does it. It's so he doesn't accidentally look at his father. So he doesn't reopen the Pandora's box that transformed their Christmas Eve from an awkward family dinner into a stroll through a minefield.

Most of the mines, however, are duds by now. Because Theodor is tired. His daily quota of reproaches and arguments has been used up. Moreover, something has been gnawing at him ever since he snapped at Kevin. Something he himself said in the heat of battle.

She needed more than me.

Those were the words. It wasn't something he had thought about beforehand. In fact, he's not sure he's ever had that thought at all. It just came out of his mouth as part of the slur that was meant to make Kevin feel guilty ... but it was himself the words hit the hardest, and they have plagued him ever since.

Because he's spent plenty of energy blaming Kevin for not doing enough when his mother got sick, but what about himself? Has he ever looked inward and examined himself with the same microscope? He claims he did everything he could ... but could he have done more?

He jolts as the car hits a road bump at too high a speed, causing the shock absorbers to screech beneath them. He turns his face to Kevin, tempted to express his unfiltered opinion about such reckless driving, but he changes his mind when realizing that they're already on the street where he lives. Then the awkward silence can be allowed to prevail a little longer.

In the end, it's Kevin who breaks it when he stops the car on the road in front of Theodor's snowy driveway.

"It turned out to be quite a night, huh?" he says. "But still, we're glad that you decided to celebrate Christmas with us, even if it's not the same as when Mom was here ... but Kimberly does what she can."

Despite the stiff smile that can be glimpsed on his lips in the semi-darkness of the car, Kevin sounds like he means it. For a moment, this makes Theodor consider if he has been unreasonable. That perhaps not *everything* his son and daughter-in-law do is motivated by an underlying, egocentric agenda.

But then Kevin opens his mouth again.

"Of course, it was probably easier for Mom to create the atmosphere. I mean, the surroundings up by the cabin kind of scream Christmas, right? Reindeer and pine trees in spades."

He hesitates for a moment and then nods as if what he is about to say has just appeared in his head.

"Maybe we should do it again someday? You know, go up to the cabin and celebrate Christmas. Like we did in the old days. I mean, it's a kind of a shame having a place like that and then not even using it, right?"

And ... there it is. Theodor feels the heat rising, first in his throat, then in his temples. He wants to scream at Kevin to knock that bloody cabin out of his head. That his dad would rather see it rot and turn into dust than sell it or, *God forbid*, give it to him and Kimberly so they can tear it down and build some sterile glass block on the grounds.

"Thanks for tonight, Kevin," he manages to limit his answer to—but apparently his tone of voice fills in the rest of the message because Kevin just clears his throat and says:

"Yeah, um ... you too, Dad."

After getting out, Theodor stays in the driveway while Kevin's Audi rolls across the snowy street and then turns left at a traffic light. Only when the red glow from its taillights is completely gone does he begin to walk toward the house. However, he only manages to take a few steps before he stops again.

What it is, he has no idea, but something is wrong. He can sense it.

He glances back to the street, checking in both directions. Doctor Pearson's flamboyant Christmas lights over on the other side really ought to be categorized as a criminal offence, but beyond that, nothing seems out of the ordinary.

He squints his eyes, scans all the bushes and trees, especially those that lie in shadows.

Nothing. What he sees most clearly is his own breath. In the freezing weather, it forms small, white clouds in front of his face every time he exhales.

More annoyed than reassured, he puts his hand in the pocket of his jacket and pulls out the house key. Then he turns back around and walks up to the front door.

No monsters leap out of the shadows as he puts the key in the lock, and none of the neighborhood's snotty brats lie in hiding to throw a snowball at his neck.

But the feeling is still there, gnawing away like a small, malicious parasite in the back of his head.

As he unpacks himself from his Christmas wrapping —hat, gloves, coat, and scarf—inside the hallway, Theodor captures his reflection in the mirror on the wall.

Wrinkles, gray hair, and almost just as gray skin. He looks old, but why shouldn't he? He has lived a long time. Too long. He wasn't supposed to be the one left behind. In a just world, it would be Martha's reflection that was thrown back right now.

The thought makes his gaze slide upward, where it finds the photo of her standing in the snow in front of the water up in Maiden Lake. In the very same place where he, at her request, spread her ashes about a year after that picture was taken.

Her smile. Oh God, how he misses that smile.

A shadow—something moving outside the frosted glass window of the front door—makes him spin around.

The shadow grows larger behind the glass, turns into a full silhouette of a man, and when it has come close enough, a blurry white hand appears in front of it and knocks on the window.

Three short taps, and then the hand pulls back, merging once more with the dark figure.

Theodor glances down at his wristwatch. It's past midnight. What the hell can be so important that it can't wait until tomorrow?

A stab of uncertainty hits him, but he shakes it off, then walks to the door and opens it slightly.

"Can I help you with something?"

The tall man outside the door smiles, then tilts his head and stares at Theodor. He does this for a long time. Too long. It's almost as if he is studying some sensational archaeological find. Then, suddenly, he nods and broadens his smile even more.

"Mr. Moody?"

"That would be me," Theodor confirms. "And you are ...?"

"Oh yeah, of course," the tall man exclaims, holding

up his hand apologetically and then sliding it inside his open jacket.

For a split second, this move causes Theodor to take a step backward, but then the man's hand reappears. What he has pulled out of his inner pocket turns out to be a leather case with an ID card on one side and a police badge on the other.

"Guess I probably should have started with that," he says. "Do forgive me. I'm a cop—plainclothes, as you can see—and I've been called out here because some of your neighbors have reported a couple of suspicious vans roaming the neighborhood. So, I'm taking a quick round talking to the residents."

Before answering, Theodor takes a second to study the ID card in the hand of the tall man. Especially the last name, Rowley, feels strangely familiar.

"Sad way to spend Christmas Eve."

The officer shrugs, baring his teeth in a smile once more.

"Somebody has to do it," he says. "But don't worry, I had my Christmas dinner with my wife and kid back home before I left."

"Well, okay, that's ... that's good," Theodor replies, slightly confused by the policeman's urge to share that information. "But I'm afraid I'm not much help, Officer. I just got home, and I didn't see no van."

"Vans," the tall man corrects. "There were two of them."

"Oh, okay, of course. But I still haven't seen them, so um ..."

He starts to pull away from the door frame to signal that the conversation is over in his eyes, but the officer doesn't go anywhere. If anything, he seems to be leaning forward slightly so his face comes closer to the crevice. His gray eyes once more carry the strange, analytical expression.

"Are you sure that everything is okay, Mr. Moody? You seem a bit on edge. Are you ... alone in there?"

"Everything is just fine," Theodor replies, now with a hint of irritation in his voice. "I'm tired after a long night, that's all. And yes, I'm alone."

The officer's face grows even bigger in the narrow crevice. It's so close now that the stubble on his cheek almost scrapes against the door frame.

"You don't have to say anything out loud," he whispers. "You can just blink your eyes twice. Then I'll know you need help."

Confused and slightly disturbed by this strange behavior, Theodor looks toward the inside of his house and then back at the policeman.

"I *don't* need any help, sir. And I think I'd like you to leave my property now."

"Oh, but I think you do, Mr. Moody," the officer says, still in the low, murmuring voice. "Maybe not from the police, but help in some form you do need. Otherwise, you wouldn't do the things that you do."

"What things?"

"Paying young women to prance around your house so you can satisfy your perversities."

Theodor blinks his eyes and shakes his head as if he had just been slapped. That's also what it feels like.

"I have to ask," the officer continues in his *we're just two buddies sharing a secret* tone of voice. "Is it enough for you to just look, or do you sneak in a little squeeze every now and then?"

His lips are still smiling, but above them, the man's eyes are small and filled with something that Theodor absolutely doesn't like.

"I have no idea what this is about, but frankly, I don't appreciate it, and I'll have to ask you to leave, Officer ..."

The two things come to him simultaneously; the officer's last name and the explanation as to why it seemed so familiar when he read it on the ID card.

Rowley. The same last name as Yuki.

For reasons he doesn't fully understand, that realization causes an icy panic to spread in him, and he instinctively starts pushing the door shut.

But it's too late. Dean Rowley's winter boot has already found its way into the crack, preventing it from closing.

CHAPTER 30

"Shit!" Yuki moans as a beam of light pours in through the basement window, blinding her.

That's the first confirmation that Plan A's deadline has expired, so Plan B must be put into action. The second confirmation is the sound of snow crunching under the tires of Dean's Raptor out in the driveway.

Plan A was the window—and ten more minutes would probably have enabled her to break the frame free. But there is no point in worrying about that now.

"Sammy, we won't make it," she says, after which she points to the basement stairs—or rather, to the dark space under the stairs.

Sammy remains silent—as he has been for quite a while now—but he must still have been paying attention when she explained the plans because he doesn't hesitate to run over and hide in the darkness under the stairs.

That's plan B. To hide under the stairs, where they have a view of the entire basement through the gaps between the steps. There, hidden in the shadows, she'll wait for Dean to come down to them. And when she can see his heels on the steps in front of her ...

She glances down at the metal pole in her hands and tightens her grip on it. She's not going to let that psychopath harm a hair on Sammy's head. Not one.

After joining her son under the stairs, she makes eye contact with him and places a finger on her lips.

He nods. He looks terrified, but that's okay. At least it confirms that he understands that Dean is a genuine threat. The situation would have been far more precarious if the boy wasn't convinced or perhaps even refused to accept that his dad could be the villain.

Up on the ground floor, a door is opened and closed again. Next follows a series of footsteps, which get louder and louder until they stop somewhere near the door to the basement.

For a moment, it's quiet, and Yuki has a thought that, even though she knows it's completely irrational, gives her a shred of hope.

Maybe he won't come down here tonight at all. Maybe he'll go straight to bed and—

A loud, insistent scraping sound rips that thought to

pieces. It's the sound of something heavy being dragged across a wooden floor. So, it was a piece of furniture—and not boards from the garage—he used to block the door.

The door creaks as he pulls it open, and a cool wind sneaks down behind the stairs, caressing the back of Yuki's neck.

Dean starts walking, and with each heavy, creaking step he takes down the stairs, dust sprinkles down and swirls around Yuki and Sammy.

Halfway down, he pauses, perhaps because he has noticed the window with the broken frame.

"Sammy?" she hears him ask into the quiet basement. "Sammy, are you still here?"

Where else would he be, you son of a bitch? You locked him in.

"Sammy, sweetie? Has Mom woken up?"

His voice is unusually tender and mild—loving, almost—and for a moment, that fills Yuki with horror. Because what if Sammy buys it? What if his innocent heart makes him forget what Dean has done?

To her relief, Sammy doesn't make a sound. He, like her, sits completely still with his eyes fixed on the one step that curves downwards a little more than the others a couple of feet above their heads. And his eyes are not those of a boy who longs for his father's embrace. They're the eyes of a boy who cautiously watches a large dog that has escaped from its collar in the park and has white foam around his mouth where the muzzle should have been.

"Is Mom awake?" Dean repeats, taking a step further down the stairs.

Yuki clenches her hands around the metal pole so hard that it hurts. One or two more steps and he'll be within her reach.

"Is Mom okay, Sammy? Answer me!"

The step just above her face creaks, and a new veil of dust sprinkles down in front of her. She sees it a bit too late, and some of it finds its way to her mouth and her nostrils.

Her body tries to force her to get it out, but she fights back with everything she's got. A sneeze or cough at this moment would be a death sentence. For her—and perhaps also for Sammy.

No sooner has she won this first battle against the instincts of her body than the next one commences. Because now, Dean takes another step, bringing the heel of his boot down to the level of her eyes.

Clusters of snow hang on the edge of the sole. But it's not white snow. It's pink. And the red tinge could very well be blood. Theodor's blood.

This time, she loses the battle. Her body's instinct—the gasp of shock—can't be held back. And once it's out, there is no turning back.

She raises the metal pole, pulls it back over her shoulder as if it were a spear ... and then she sends it full force through the gap between the steps. Directly into her husband's left calf muscle.

Both the feeling and the sound are dreadful. She can feel the pole's tip meeting brief resistance, probably tendon strands, before sliding effortlessly into the muscle. And the sound, oh God, it's the same sucking sound that Sammy's toy gecko used to make when the suction cups under its feet were pulled off the window in the living room.

Dean lets out a roar of pain and tumbles forward down the stairs. The pull rips the pole out of Yuki's hands. It follows him for a short distance but is stopped abruptly when it hits the lower edge of the step above it.

This collision creates a counter pull that rips the pole out of the muscle again and sends a barrage of small drops of blood into Yuki's face.

Meanwhile, Dean lets out another cry of pain—and even now, falling, bleeding, and roaring in pain, he finds the energy to weave in a threat into his wife.

"I'LL KILL YOU, YOU LITTLE BITCH!" he roars as he hits the concrete floor, first with his knees, then with his hands and face.

Aware that she can't afford to waste a single second, Yuki leaps out from hiding, grabs the metal pole, and hammers it down on Dean's back.

Again and again, she brings it down on him, hard and mercilessly. She screams as she does it. Threats and curses that have lain beneath the surface of her consciousness, suppressed for years, pour out of her mouth as if they were toxic substances her body was trying to expel. In a way, they are.

But despite her anger, despite her newfound cold-bloodedness, the man at her feet is still a giant compared to her. A monster whose genes would have invited a career in wrestling or football if the police academy hadn't caught his eye. And even though the blows are raining down on him, he is still conscious—and he's slowly but surely moving his hands to the sides so that he can lean on the floor and press himself upwards.

"You'd better make sure that I never get up," he snarls as he pushes and lifts the first five inches of what should be an impossible push-up. "Otherwise, you'll be very sorry when I get a hold of you."

Small shots of panic, like electrical impulses, rush through her body at that threat, and the urge to let go of the weapon and flee up the stairs is starting to overwhelm her. It's just not an option. Dean is much bigger and much faster than both her and Sammy, so she has to get the car keys from him. And to do that, she'll need to knock him out cold.

The problem is that it's starting to feel like an impossible task.

Barely is this thought completed before she picks up a movement out of the corner of her eyes. Something white, flying through the air.

Only when the bottom of the paint bucket hits Dean in the back of the head and then topples sideways, causing a pool of thick white paint to spread on the floor, does she realize what has happened.

Sammy has come to her rescue by throwing a half-full, five-gallon paint bucket at his father's head—and this time, Dean's left cheek stays flat against the floor after hitting it.

"Up there, Sammy," Yuki says, pointing to the basement door at the end of the stairs. "Now!"

For a moment, nothing happens. The boy just stands there, his eyes flickering back and forth between the paint bucket and Dean. As if he is unable to understand what he has just done. Then he suddenly awakens with a start and follows his mother's orders.

As Sammy runs up the stairs, Yuki crouches next to Dean's unconscious body. The truck keys are in the pocket of his jeans, she can see the outline of the bundle through the fabric ... but his hand, his huge hand, lies on the floor right next to it, less than ten inches from his pocket. If it suddenly reaches for her ...

The longer you hesitate, the greater the chance that he will wake up, she scolds herself in her mind. *So, stop stalling and take those keys!*

She pulls in a mouthful of air and holds it in as she stretches out her hand and slides two of her fingers down behind the edge of his pocket.

She wasn't wrong. The truck key is down there. She

can feel the rubber coating and the smooth part where the logo sits. But she can also feel the warmth from Dean's body and the pressure of the fabric. It feels unsafe, like a trap that will close and lock her fingers in at any moment.

She shuts her eyes, closes her fingertips around one of the keys, and pulls carefully. When she opens them again, she sits with the keychain in her lap, and her husband's big hand is still lying limply on the floor.

She pushes herself up and glances back over her shoulder. Sammy is still up there, one foot on the highest step of the stairs and one on the floor of the hallway on the ground floor.

Slowly, and with half an eye on Dean, she moves up the stairs. When she reaches Sammy, she pauses and pulls him close.

What she really wants to say is that it's going to be okay and that she loves him. But she knows she'll break down if she does that. So instead, she grabs his shoulders firmly and looks at him.

"I've got the truck keys," she whispers. "But we still need to be quiet, okay?"

Sammy sniffles and nods.

"Good, then let's get out of here."

With those words, she leads him past the dark wooden sideboard that normally resides in the living room—it was what Dean used to block off the basement door. When they've passed it, they continue through the house. Only once do they stop, and that's just to put on their jackets and boots before stepping out into the freezing driveway.

Under their feet, the snow crunches treacherously, and when the wind picks up, a thin layer of snow is pulled off the top of the hedge and swirls over them.

With fingers quivering so badly that it's almost impossible, Yuki puts the key in the door and unlocks the pickup. At least Dean has just been out driving, so she doesn't have to remove a layer of ice first, which is often the case at this time of year.

She opens the door and starts to get in, but pauses when she spots Sammy.

He is standing on the running board on the other side with his hand on the roof of the truck, either trying to pull himself together or retreating into a more pleasant place than the current reality.

"Sammy!" she says, a little too sharply, while she knocks on the truck roof. "We have to get going, sweetie. Before he ... before he wakes up, okay?"

As an unpleasant confirmation of those words, a rattling sound emerges from somewhere behind them.

Maybe nothing. Maybe Dean coming up from the basement.

Sammy jerks his head from side to side as if the sound has woken him. Then he nods to his mother and gets in the truck.

Inside the vehicle, Yuki once again has to fight her

shaking hands—first to get the seat belt clicked in the buckle, next to get the key in the ignition.

"Mom, come on!" Sammy says. Anxious, but not angry. "We need to go!"

She nods, turns the key, and for a split second, she is convinced that the car won't start. That it has somehow been brought to life and now, like a protective pet, takes the side of its owner.

The animal growls ... but then starts to purr.

She looks backward, begins to back out of the driveway, looks forward again, and—

He is there. A large, night-black silhouette in the center of the doorway into the hallway, framed by a yellow square of light. The creature from the nightmare that has been going on for almost half of her life.

"W-what's that in his hand?" Sammy asks, but before Yuki can even focus on the object, it's already airborne. It hits the windshield with a screech, leaving a furrowed white crack, before continuing across the roof of the truck and disappearing into the darkness. There is a remnant left, though; a cylinder of cloth that now rolls through the cones from the headlights and across the driveway as if it were tumbleweed in a desert.

It's the shade from the lamp that was on the sideboard that Dean used to block the basement door. He must have grabbed it on his way out here.

"YOU BITCH!" he yells as he speeds up and stomps

across the snow. "DON'T YOU DARE DRIVE AWAY FROM ME!"

Yuki steps on the gas pedal and turns the steering wheel sharply to the right as soon as the vehicle is clear of the driveway—but the road is far more slippery than she had expected, and the back end starts to fishtail. She slams on the brakes, overcorrects, and the truck drifts in a semicircle and only stops when it faces the sidewalk on the opposite side.

"No, no, no!" she chants, while she steps on the gas pedal once more—only to feel the wheels spin uselessly beneath the vehicle.

Meanwhile, Dean is getting closer and closer. Ten more feet, and he'll be right by Sammy's window.

"Come on. Oh God, come on!"

A relief, deep and intense, cascades through her when the wheels suddenly get a grip on the road and pull the vehicle forward just before Dean's hand touches the window.

But her relief is short-lived, for although her husband's silhouette is now getting smaller and smaller in the rear window, his threat still reaches her ears.

"I WILL FIND YOU, YUKI! TRUST ME! AND WHEN I DO ..."

CHAPTER 31

To the uninformed observer on this late Christmas night, the sight of Theodor's house on Rue Lane probably wouldn't be a cause for alarm.

If, on the other hand, one is aware that something is wrong, it isn't difficult to spot the signs of danger. Thus, Yuki instantly registers the two different sets of footprints in the driveway, and she notices the front door, which should be closed but is halfway open, swaying slightly back and forth as the wind pulls on it.

"As soon as I'm out, you lock the doors."

Sammy stares at her for a moment. Then he shakes his head.

"I'm coming with you."

"Sammy, I ... I don't know if that's a good idea."

"I'm coming with you!" the boy repeats sharply.

Yuki sighs but ends up nodding.

"Okay. But you stay behind me. And if I tell you to do something, you do it. No negotiations. Got it?"

"Got it."

With the exception of the wind's unsettling wails, it's completely silent outside. Under normal circumstances, this would probably be a charming neighborhood at this late hour, perfect for a stroll under the warm glow of the streetlamps. Right now, however, it's intimidating. Especially since the pink cluster of snow on Dean's boots has given her a clear expectation of what they are going to find behind the half-open front door.

That feeling only grows stronger as they reach the door and a new sound joins the wind.

The grandfather clock. Theodor's old grandfather clock, which is located in his living room, but whose heavy ticking can be heard all throughout the house—and apparently also out here.

She can't put her finger on why, but that sound has the hairs on her neck standing up. Maybe it's because it sounds so harrowing. So ... final.

She pushes the door gently with the tip of her boot and looks inside.

The hallway is empty, but something bad has definitely happened there. The mirror on the wall is slanted, and on the floor lies a crumpled-up jacket.

"Theodor?"

Nothing. Only the constant ticking from the grandfather clock.

She raises a hand to tell Sammy to stay in the doorway. Then she goes into the hallway and from there into the kitchen.

She turns on the light, scans the room, and feels her mouth dry out.

Theodor isn't in here either, but there's a fair chance the bloody handprints on the floor and two of the bottom cupboards could be his.

Oh no, Dean. What have you done?

The floor creaks behind her, and she spins around in one swift motion.

"What is it, Mom?" asks Sammy, who has defied her orders and is now standing in the middle of the hallway. He is pale, obviously terrified of what she's going to answer.

"Nothing," she says as convincingly as she can. "He's not in the kitchen."

Sammy nods, looking like he doesn't know whether to be relieved or troubled by that information. Truth be told, she doesn't know either.

"I'll check the living room," she whispers. "And this time you stay put. Is that clear?"

Sammy doesn't answer, but he doesn't move his feet either.

Even before crossing the threshold into the room, she instinctively knows that this is where she'll find Theodor.

Not only can she see that there has been a commotion in there—more than one piece of furniture has been pushed around and some have tipped over—she can also smell it. She can smell sweat, and she can smell blood.

His hand, sticking out behind the couch, is the first thing she spots. It lies limply on the floor, fingers curled and red with dried blood.

As she rounds the corner of the couch, the rest of the macabre sight unfolds before her, and the shock triggers a sour reflux, nearly making her vomit.

His face is swollen. Uneven lines of blood run from the corner of his mouth and his nostrils down one cheek.

"Oh no, Theodor," she moans as she falls to her knees next to him and places a hand gently on his cheek.

It's hot. Thank God, his cheek is hot.

"Sammy, get in here and help me!"

"Did you find him? Is he okay?"

"He will be, but ... you should know that he's pretty banged up."

She barely has time to finish the sentence before Sammy comes rushing into the living room at such a high speed that he almost collides with the armrest of the couch before stopping—and turning pale.

"Did Dad do this?"

Yuki bites her lip and answers the question with a

small nod ... but she can't bring herself to look up and meet his gaze while doing so.

"Help me get him up," she says, and as Sammy kneels on the floor, she once again puts her hand on Theodor's cheek.

"Theodor? It's Yuki. Can you hear me?"

For a moment, it's quiet. Then Theodor makes a strained swallowing motion and opens his eyes. He looks at her, but it seems like he's having trouble focusing.

"Yuki?"

"I'm here, Theodor," she says, after which she looks over at Sammy and corrects herself. "*We're* here."

Theodor looks down at his hand, turns it around so the palm is face up, and then slides it across the floor until it's next to Sammy.

The boy takes it in his own and gives it a squeeze that says as much as any words would have.

"I was ... attacked?" Theodor says, glancing around the chaotic mess surrounding them in the living room. As if he needs to verify the truth in his own words. "I don't even know what he ..."

Suddenly, he opens his eyes wide and turns his face toward Yuki.

"He was a cop. It was—"

"My husband," Yuki finishes for him. "I know. And I'm so sorry you've been dragged into this."

"My dad is sick," Sammy elaborates.

Hearing the boy repeat her own words like that brings tears to Yuki's eyes, and she turns her face away until she has it under control again.

Theodor sees her doing it, but he doesn't comment on it—which she is grateful for. Especially since the question *is* in there. She can read it in his eyes, above his swollen cheeks.

"We have to get you to a hospital," she says.

"Not before I get some answers."

"I'm serious, Theodor. You should see yourself."

He doesn't respond with words, but she notices his gaze drifting down to the bruises on her forearm—a gift from her otherwise cautious husband when he wrapped her in the Christmas tablecloth and swung her around the room like a rag doll.

"Sammy, do me a favor and get a couple of pillows from the bedroom so we can sit him up, will you?"

The boy nods and pushes himself up.

"I'll be right back."

Theodor tries to show his gratitude with a smile, but the result is a strained grimace that looks more anguished than grateful.

"It's nice of you, kiddo. Thank you."

With Sammy gone, Theodor directs his drowsy, flickering gaze at Yuki—and then the question he held back earlier is articulated.

"It's not the first time, is it?"

"No," Yuki sighs—and after a long pause, she adds, "But it will be the last."

"And Sammy? Did your husband also ...?"

"Never!" Yuki spits out, almost like an automatic defense mechanism. Then it hits her how much the events of this one Christmas Eve have changed her life. For good.

"Not ... not before today," she continues. "This is the first time Dean has let Sammy see what he, um ... what he's really like."

An image, brief but terrible, flickers before her mind's eye—Dean's dark silhouette appearing in the doorway as they backed out of the driveway—and she buries her face in her hands.

"But it wasn't just that he didn't hide it from Sammy this time. There was something else. He was ... *hateful*. More than I've ever seen before. I don't know why. If we hadn't gotten away, I don't know what would have happened. What he would have done to us."

Neither of the last three sentences is entirely true. Yuki knows perfectly well why Dean was different. His empty-headed goose of a wife had defied him and deceived him. *Humiliated* him. So now the stakes had to be raised as compensation for the secrets she had hidden in the HOTHEADS box.

And the other untruth? Yuki knows, in her heart and soul, exactly what Dean would have done if they hadn't escaped. Her only possible doubt is whether he would have dragged it out or not.

"Oh God, Theodor. I'm so terribly sorry about this."

"Stop it. What happened, happened. Right now, we've got to keep our heads cool. Is he going to come back? Your husband, I mean. Will he come back here to look for you?"

The question hits her like a punch to the stomach. How could she not have considered that?

"We, um ... took his truck, so he'll have to find another, but ..."

"But he will come back here?"

She gives him an anxious look and nods.

"And did you call the police?"

"There wasn't time, and we don't have our phones," she says, shrugging. "But it wouldn't help, anyway."

"What do you mean?"

"Dean is a cop. They have each other's backs. He made a point of telling me that so I wouldn't get any bright ideas. He always says that there are no *colleagues* in the police force. There are only *brothers*."

"Will these work?" a bright voice asks behind her, but before she can answer, Theodor preempts her.

"They're fine, Sammy."

The boy smiles and hurries over to them, a pillow under each arm.

Grunting in pain—and with the support of both of them—Theodor struggles his way up into a sitting posi-

261

tion, leaning against the coffee table and using Sammy's two cushions as backrests.

"Is it bad?" Sammy asks.

Theodor, who is now high enough up to catch his own reflection on the television screen opposite the couch, contorts his face and sighs.

"I don't think I'll be winning any beauty pageants in the near future," he grunts. "But other than that, it's okay. I'm still alive."

He looks down at his legs and blows air out of his nostrils with a hissing sound.

"Give me a moment to catch my breath, then I'll be ready to get all the way up."

Sammy looks at his mother, who nods and gives him a frozen smile.

"We've got no other choice," she says. "We can't stay here much longer, nor can we leave Theodor here by himself. He needs to go to a hospital."

"I'm a grown man," Theodor objects. "I'll decide for myself whether I'm going to the doctor or not. And right now, there are more important things to take care of than my old bones. Right now, all we need to worry about is getting out of here."

With a good deal of gratitude, Yuki accepts his decision. And to her surprise, Sammy does the same. She had expected him to protest and demand that they call an ambulance for Theodor, but he simply nods.

"Are you ready?"

The old man lets out a disgruntled groan. That's answer enough for Yuki, who lifts his arm up on her shoulder and gestures for Sammy to do the same.

All things considered, it's a success. They get Theodor to his feet, and after a short rest, he also manages to use them to walk across the living room.

"Sammy, could you run into the kitchen and get my cell phone? It's in the little gray basket next to the newspaper rack."

"I'll get it!" Yuki exclaims, almost throwing herself in front of Sammy to make sure he doesn't slip past her. "Then you can help Theodor outside in the meantime."

One could argue that it's pointless, especially since Sammy has already seen how badly Theodor is hurt. Still, Yuki doesn't want to send him into the kitchen. Those blood-red handprints on the cupboards ... there was just something really disturbing about them.

For the same reason, she doesn't spend any more time in there now than what is absolutely necessary. She locates the gray basket and grabs the cell phone—which mostly looks like an old-fashioned pocket calendar because it's wrapped in the thick, brown leather casing that people over sixty seem to prefer.

By the time she returns, the other two have already made it to the hallway, and Sammy is helping Theodor put on his shoes.

"Do you have a place to stay tonight?" Theodor asks. "Family, or ...?"

Yuki feels the hopelessness creeping in. She had the same question circling in the back of her mind on the way over here. And the answer is still just as discouraging.

Without the contents of the HOTHEADS box, there's no place where Dean won't find her within a very short amount of time. That was the whole point of putting that money aside every month. Getting so far away that none of the strings Dean would normally pull could lead him to her and Sammy.

She answers Theodor's question by shaking her head and muttering: "There's no place where Dean won't find us ... and he *will* try."

For a long time, Theodor stares at her with a strange, brooding expression in his eyes. Then he lets out a rusty sigh and looks up at the shelf above the mirror.

"I might have a place," he says. "But if we go up there, I want you to promise me something."

Yuki squints her eyes but says nothing.

"It's probably too late now, it being Christmas Eve night and all," Theodor continues. "But first thing tomorrow, you'll contact a crisis center that deals with domestic violence. They have experience with things like this, and they can help you and Sammy far better than I can."

For a while, Yuki continues to stare at him, not quite knowing what his point really is. Then it hits her, and she nods.

"You have my word," she says—making sure to look him in the eyes so he understands that it's not just an empty promise. That she's not going to stick her tail between her legs and crawl back to her abusive husband as soon as the adrenaline—and the courage along with it—has left her body.

Because she isn't.

Not this time.

CHAPTER 32

It's this exact feeling that Theodor has been trying to avoid. The feeling of being gripped by the cold, bony fingers of grief and pulled back under the surface of the water.

In actual fact, he's been out of the water for almost two years, but at this moment, it feels like he's only just been up long enough to get in half a mouthful of oxygen.

How can something so beautiful hurt so much?

Maiden Lake is the name of both the lake and the area surrounding it. And it *is* beautiful; tall, snow-capped mountains with scattered clusters of pine trees, deep valleys with enough peace and quiet to lure in a wealth of wildlife.

And at the center of it all, the lake. A glossy, drop-shaped water surface that during the day makes it seem as if a piece of the blue sky has fallen to the ground—and that at night gives the moon a twin sister.

"It's like something out of a Disney film," he hears Yuki whisper in the driver's seat. "I can't believe how beautiful it is."

Whether she's actually making conversation or just thinking out loud, Theodor isn't sure, but he chooses to go with the former. Partly because it gives him a welcome opening to divert his own thoughts.

"Martha used to say the same," he says in the same hushed voice as Yuki so he doesn't wake up Sammy, who went out like a light in the back seat half an hour ago. "She always said she felt like Snow White surrounded by the animals of the forest when we went for walks up here."

A memory suddenly emerges in his mind, and despite his grief, he feels his lips forming a smile.

"She also always said it made her want to burst into song ... but that she never did out of fear of being arrested for animal cruelty."

Yuki makes a half-choked, sputtering sound and looks at him with wide eyes as if to say: *Really? She said that?*

"And the worst part is that she was probably right," Theodor says, nodding. "God knows I adored that woman, but she couldn't carry a tune if her life depended on it."

"She sounds lovely, your wife."

"She was. An optimist to the bone."

After those words, Theodor turns to the window at his side and stares blankly at the landscape gliding by behind his reflection.

In many ways, this mirror feels truer than any other ever has. Because that's what it feels like inside his head. As if an endless series of memories of this place keep sliding by. And just like the landscape in the moonlight outside, the images in his mind are blurred and move too fast for him to capture the details.

"I ... spread her ashes up here," he suddenly says. "She made me promise that."

Silence. Then Yuki takes her hand off the steering wheel for a moment and gives his shoulder a gentle squeeze.

"I want to thank you, Theodor."

He looks at her, tries to read her face, but it's difficult because in the night sky above them, the moon has crawled into hiding behind a gray cloud, so her eyes lie in darkness.

"I can see how hard it is for you to come up here," she continues. "And yet you're doing it now, for me and Sammy."

Theodor opens his mouth ... and then closes it again without saying anything.

Yuki is apparently also done talking for now. At any rate, she shifts her focus to what's on the other side of the windshield. They're only a few miles from the cabin now, which means that the asphalt road will soon be replaced with a graveled one. Not that it makes much difference, since there's a layer of snow covering everything anyhow.

For quite a while, she sits like that, staring absentmindedly at the circles of light in front of the car as if they were a hypnotist's pendulum. It's only when Sammy moans and jerks uneasily in the back seat that she wakes up and returns to the present.

"This ... is just so wrong," she says in a voice that's shaky and troubled. "This wasn't how it was supposed to go, at all."

"How what was supposed to go?"

Yuki tilts her head forward for a moment as if she's going to rest it on the steering wheel. Then she sighs and leans back.

"I was planning on leaving him. I've been putting money aside every month for a year and a half, and I only needed a few more months. Sammy's birthday in June—that was my deadline. By then, we would have had enough money to get by."

"But ...?"

"But I was a fool. I hadn't hidden the money well enough. Dean found it."

"And that's what triggered his rage tonight?"

The moon is back in the sky above them, so when Yuki turns toward him, Theodor sees both the dread and the gravity on her face clearly.

"Dean has a bad temper," she says. "But that's not his worst trait."

"What do you mean?"

"I hid the money in a matchbox down in the basement."

"Yeah?"

"He gave Sammy that matchbox tonight, as an early Christmas present. Nicely wrapped and all."

"So, he ... planned it?"

Yuki responds with a nod and trembles as if a cold breeze has just hit her.

"Yup. That's my husband. He doesn't like surprises, but he loves to surprise others. Laying traps. It makes him feel powerful, I think."

As if his subconscious has listened in and wants to concur with that interpretation, the sleeping boy in the back seat jerks uneasily, letting out a: "Uh-huh."

"Why his birthday?" Theodor asks. "Your deadline, I mean."

"Because that's when I made the decision to leave Dean. On Sammy's birthday almost two years ago."

"Because he ... hurt you?"

"Yeah, but not physically. That day he showed me what would happen if I stayed."

She hesitates as if considering whether to continue. Then she nods to herself.

"Really, it was a small thing. We had invited guests, nothing big, just a group of Sammy's friends from his school. One of them was a girl, Lisa Mulligan, who has been in Sammy's class since they were little. During the party, she accidentally knocked over a glass of soda, soaking one of Sammy's gifts, and he got very angry about it. He ..."

She hesitates again, and her lips tremble a little.

"He called her a brainless goose and said that he never should have invited a girl because girls don't know how to do anything right. I believe his exact wording was that girls couldn't hammer a nail in a turd without breaking both."

"And I can almost guess where he's heard that kind of talk," Theodor says.

Yuki nods bitterly.

"The worst part was that his dad was right next to him. And you know what he did?"

"Nothing?"

"Worse. He winked at him and gave him a pat on the back. His son had just called a girl a useless goose, and Dean responded with a pat on the back. At that moment, I realized I had to get Sammy away so he wouldn't end up like his dad."

What deep, philosophical words one says in the wake of such a story, Martha would surely have known. Theodor, on the other hand, hasn't got the faintest idea. Therefore, it's a relief for him that his escape is found in the familiar surroundings outside the vehicle.

"There's a side road coming up after the next bend,"

he says, pointing. "It's marked with a yellow sign. If it's still there, that is."

The sign is still there, and when Yuki sees it, she lets out a loud sigh.

"It's hard not to think that the universe must have a sense of irony."

"What do you mean?" Theodor asks, but even before she opens her mouth, he has seen it too.

ROUGH ROAD AHEAD is what is written on the sign.

CHAPTER 33

After turning off the engine on Dean's Raptor, Yuki doesn't get out of the truck right away. Instead, she stays in the driver's seat for a moment, absorbing—and processing—her impressions of the place.

The cabin isn't overly large, but it's just as charming as she imagined it to be, based on the photographs in Theodor's house. Even with the moon's sparse light as the only source of illumination, that's an obvious fact.

It's a log cabin with a thatched roof and a long, covered wooden terrace out front. At the foot of this begins a slope that leads down to the shore of the lake, and on the other side of the cabin is a wooded area that stretches a good way up the mountainside.

"You haven't considered renting it out?" Yuki asks. "With these surroundings, it must be a gold mine."

"I'm sure my son would agree," Theodor says. "But

no, the area around the lake is protected, and it was a struggle just to be allowed to keep the land. So, to acquire a license for renting ..."

He shrugs and gives her a wry smile.

"That's the official explanation. The unofficial is that I actually do have one paying guest who comes up here once or twice a year."

"Oh, really? Even after, um ..."

"Yes, it might be silly to keep doing it, but it was something Martha arranged back in the day, and he came up here so often that we ended up giving him his own key. So, there's not really any hassle in it for me. He even keeps a ledger and wires the money once a year. He's an author and he comes up here to write."

"Still, it's nice of you to let him keep doing it," Yuki says, and inside herself, she adds: *You're full of surprises, Mr. Moody.*

"Nah," Theodor says. "Martha loved his books, so for her, it was kind of fun, and ... I don't know. Shall we?"

"What? Yeah, of course. Can you walk by yourself, or do you need a hand?"

"Don't worry, I'm fine," Theodor says, nodding toward Sammy in the back seat. "If you wake him up, I'll light the fireplace in the meantime."

It's an old man's pride talking—that's revealed by the way he clutches his ribs and contorts his face as he gets out—but Yuki decides to let it slide. If it gets too bad, he'll let her know.

"Sammy, sweetie? We're at Theodor's cabin."

She reaches her arm in between the seats and gives the boy's knees a gentle push.

"What?" he mumbles.

"We're here, sweetie. We've arrived at Theodor's cabin."

Slowly, the boy opens his eyes and looks at her. For the first few seconds, there is only confusion on his face. Then the realization hits, and Yuki's heart feels like it's about to burst. Because she knows exactly what thought she glimpsed in his eyes.

Oh no, it wasn't just a dream.

"Theodor?" he asks.

"He went ahead, to turn on the heat ... and he feels better. Should we go find him?"

Sammy nods but still just sits limply in the back seat with his drowsy eyes aimed at nothing.

"Hey, sweetie. One of your shoelaces is untied."

Sammy looks down, nods ... and looks completely broken at the thought of having to lean all the way down there to fix it.

"Oh my, you're really gone, huh?" Yuki says, after which she gets out of the truck and opens the door into the backseat. "Give me your foot and I'll fix it."

Sammy moves his foot toward her, and she leans down, grabs the two ends of the lace, and ties his shoes—just like she did in the first many years of his life.

"Thanks, Mom." He closes his eyes, hesitates for a moment, opens them again, and then adds, "I love you."

"I love you too, sweetie," Yuki says, and for the first time since this Christmas Eve turned into a living hell, she allows herself to feel hopeful. Because Sammy is still her beautiful, kind-hearted little boy—and as long as that holds true, there is hope.

And now they're away from Dean, so everything is going to be okay.

Five inches. That's all it would have taken to tear that thought to pieces. Had Yuki leaned just five inches farther down when she tied Sammy's shoelaces, she would have spotted it.

The little black box under the seat.

Dean's GPS tracker.

PART VII
THE FORT

"Old age isn't so bad,
considering the alternative."

THINGS MARTHA USED TO SAY

CHAPTER 34

"It's quite, um ... different, huh, sweetie?"

Sammy tilts his head and shrugs as if to say, *doesn't bother me.*

And clearly, it doesn't, because the boy shovels in one mouthful after another at breakneck speed. Yuki, on the other hand, struggles a bit to convince both her brain and her stomach that canned spaghetti in tomato sauce is a suitable breakfast meal. But then again, she should probably just be thankful that there *was* food to be found in the pantry at all, seeing as their host didn't exactly have time to prepare for the visit.

"How were the guest beds?" that very same host asks from his seat on the couch. "Did you sleep okay?"

"It took a while for us to fall asleep," Yuki replies. "But I think that's always the case with new places. Unfamiliar sounds, you know."

And being on the run from a violent psychopath, she adds inside of herself. *That doesn't help either.*

"I heard a wolf," Sammy exclaims.

"You *think* you heard a wolf," Yuki corrects.

"It was howling. What else would it be?"

"An owl?"

"Ha-ha, you're so funny."

"Thank you, I try."

With those words, Yuki gets up from the table and walks over to Theodor in the living room.

Oh, well, calling it the living room is a bit broad, since the cabin's three largest rooms—the sofa room, the kitchen, and the dining room—are grouped in one area and only separated by two half-walls.

In addition to this three-in-one room, there is a guest room with two beds, a bathroom, a pantry, and the master bedroom, housing a double bed. So, all in all, seven rooms, all filled with the smell of pine and dust.

"Later today, we can take a trip to Ullborough," Theodor says, as Yuki takes a seat next to him on the couch. "It's the nearest town with shops. Nothing fancy, just a small grocery store, but they have the bare necessities."

Yuki nods and then glances over at Sammy. He is still sitting at the table with his attention directed at the spaghetti dish.

Good. She leans closer to Theodor and lowers her voice to a whisper.

"It would be good if we could also find a little something for him. It's Christmas morning, and all his presents are under the tree at home."

"Don't worry," Theodor whispers, winking at her. "I've got that covered. There's a thing down by the lake that I think he'll like."

Maybe it's just the surprise, or maybe it's because someone other than herself has put Sammy first for once. Whatever the reason, Theodor's unexpected kindness makes her hide her face in her hands and weep.

"The only thing you have to worry about today is keeping your promise and calling a crisis center," he says softly. "You can use my cell phone. It's charging on the bedside table in my room. The coverage isn't great up here, but you can usually get a few bars outside behind the cabin."

"T-thank you," she stutters.

Theodor doesn't answer; he simply leans in toward her for a moment so their shoulders brush against each other. Then he turns his attention to Sammy.

"When you're done eating me out of the house, I've got a surprise for you, kid."

"Oh yeah? What is it?"

"A surprise, I just said that. Just finish up and we'll go out there afterward."

"Aha. So, it's outside?"

"Eat!"

Sammy obeys, and before long, a few red stripes on his plate are all that's left of the atypical breakfast. "Just leave it in the sink. I'll clean it. Then you can put on your jacket in the meantime."

"Thank you, Mom," Sammy says, after which he turns his gaze to Theodor.

Theodor raises his hand in a *yep, I'm coming* gesture and then pushes himself up from the couch. He still moans and groans a bit, Yuki notices, but he seems much better than last night. He is, she concludes as she rinses tomato sauce off the plate, a pretty tough old dog.

CHAPTER 35

"We're here," Theodor declares, knowing full and well that Sammy must be pretty confused. "Merry Christmas, kid."

Sammy looks to the sides and then back at their footprints in the snow, which draw a trail all the way up the slope, ending at the cabin door. Then he looks straight ahead again, out over the water's large, frozen surface.

"What? The lake?"

Theodor responds with a cryptic smile and then glances up at a cluster of trees standing on a mound along the lake's shore, fifteen or twenty yards to their right.

Sammy follows his gaze, scans the area ... and then he sees it.

"Oh, that's so *cool*!"

He looks at Theodor, receives a nod, and then he's gone.

The fort consists of two playhouses built in separate trees and connected to each other via a small rope bridge. Both houses hang relatively high up, about twelve feet from the ground, and to get up to them, one will have to use the rope ladder that's bolted to the floor under the door of the house to the right.

Locating the rope ladder in question didn't take Sammy long. In fact, he's already halfway to the top.

"Easy! I don't want trouble with your mother!"

"Okay!" Sammy replies, but he adjusts neither pace nor level of caution.

But that's okay. Theodor is just relieved that his idea didn't fall flat. After all, there was no way of knowing whether a fort in the treetops would excite a boy from the screen-poking generation.

Kevin loved it too, back when Theodor built it for him. That was a long time ago. He wonders whether Kevin even remembers all the hours he spent up there. And whether Kevin and Kimberly would let the fort stay if Theodor one day were to cave in and let them take over the place. Or would they tear it down along with the rest when they scrapped the cabin and put up some designer glass house in its place?

A cry of excitement sounds from the trees, and Theodor is pretty sure he knows what causes it.

Two seconds later, his notion is confirmed when Sammy steps out onto the small platform that surrounds the playhouse nearest to the lake. In his arms, he holds a rolled-up rope of the type typically used to moor boats. One end is tied to a large branch behind the fort. The other unfolds and ends up dangling three feet above the ground when Sammy drops it and lets the roll fall over the edge.

"When my son was your age, he used the rope to swing out over the lake and jump into the water," Theodor says. "Though, I wouldn't recommend trying that at this time of year."

Sammy widens his eyes and stares out over the frozen forest lake, clearly fascinated—and frightened—by the idea of using the rope as a launcher for a head dive.

"Have you ever heard ice sing?"

Sammy shakes his head, and Theodor snorts.

"Nah, it figures. A big city kid like you. Come down here for a moment and I'll show you."

While Sammy crosses the rope bridge and then climbs down the ladder, Theodor strolls down to the lake's shore to find some suitable ammunition.

He locates a rock between the stems of a reed plant protruding from the ice at the edge where water and ground meet.

Medium-sized, not too many edges. Perfect for the purpose.

"Now, it doesn't always work," he says, as Sammy catches up with him. "But I should think that the ice has the ideal thickness right now."

As he speaks, he hands the rock to Sammy. The boy takes it, but he looks skeptical—as if he's not sure if the old man is pulling his leg.

"Well, what are you waiting for? Throw it."

"Out there?"

"Yep, out on the ice. Close to the surface. Like when you're skipping rocks."

Sammy shakes his head a little reluctantly, and the skeptical expression on his face only becomes more pronounced. But the instant the rock hits the surface, that expression is washed off. In its place enters a wide smile.

The sound isn't just one sound but a series of different ones that layer on top of each other. First, it's a deep rumble, like the humming of a didgeridoo during an Aboriginal ritual. Next comes a series of short-lived, shrill sounds that mostly resemble the spaceships' laser cannons in the old *Star Wars* movies that Kevin used to love so much. Finally, the entire concert ends with a bubbling sound that travels from the point of impact to where the rock has stopped.

"What is it that makes that sound?" Sammy asks.

"I don't know. I guess the rock hitting the surface causes vibrations below."

"Wicked. Can I try again?"

"Knock yourself out."

While the boy scans the area for more rocks, Theodor walks over to a large tree stump and sits down. His body feels better than yesterday, but he sees no reason to abuse it unnecessarily.

Ironically, he's only just finished that thought before fishing out a cigarette from his pocket and lighting it.

"What is he doing?" sounds behind him.

"Looking for rocks. I showed him that ice can sing."

"Aha. And that's not the only thing you've shown him, I see. Is it safe?"

"The fort? Yeah, it's safe. Did you make the call?"

"Yep. Saints & Sisters in Swan Creek. A shelter for women in, um ... well, women like me. They were really nice."

"And?"

"And they'll have two beds available at the end of the day."

"Oh, today? W-well, okay ... that's perfect," Theodor replies, and to his surprise, he both hears and feels his own disappointment. "Then things are looking up for you."

"Yeah," Yuki replies, staring thoughtfully out over the lake where Sammy has just sent a rock flying. "Yeah, I guess they are."

"Hi, Mom!"

"Hi, sweetie!"

"Did you see the fort?"

"Yeah, it looks great. But you have to—"

"Be careful. I know!"

"That kid will be the end of me someday," Yuki sighs, after which she gently taps Theodor's arm. "Scooch over."

He obeys, and when he has done so, she takes a seat next to him on the stump.

For a long time, they sit there, doing nothing but thinking deep thoughts and watching Sammy as he throws another handful of rocks over the ice and then runs back to the fort. Although the focal points of their deep thoughts are probably comparable—their respective partners—Theodor has the feeling that the emotions they generate are very different.

Perhaps Yuki has had a similar notion. In any case, at some point, she turns her head and looks at him.

"Where was it you spread your wife's ashes? You said she wanted it done up here, right? Was it somewhere in particular?"

Theodor nods, raises his hand, and points with the two fingers holding the cigarette.

"Do you see the gorge between the two cliffs over there? You can't see it from this angle, but there's a big magnolia tree in there. Martha loved that tree. In the spring, she would sit under it for hours, buried in a book. And well, since it was her favorite place ..."

"That's where she wanted to spend eternity," Yuki finishes for him. "That's beautiful."

Theodor nods and opens his mouth to agree with her, but before he can say anything, he is interrupted by a sharp crack—the unmistakable sound of a piece of wood breaking.

It's coming from the fort.

CHAPTER 36

In reality, it's a matter of seconds, but from the moment Yuki turns her head toward the sound—and sees the board give way beneath Sammy's feet—each of those seconds feels like an eternity.

Driven by instinct—but at the same time aware that it's in vain—she jumps up from the tree stump and throws herself forward, arms and hands outstretched. Meanwhile, her boy falls to the ground—in slow motion and far beyond her reach.

She sees him reach for the edge of the platform, sees him fail, sees him being turned around in the air so he's upside down. So he'll ... oh God, so he'll hit the hard, frozen ground neck first.

Beneath her, she feels her foot slipping sideways as it hits the surface of a frozen puddle, and she stumbles helplessly forward.

And there—at the moment when her fall forces her gaze downward so she can't see Sammy—she hears it. The sound of something hitting the ground with a short, muffled crunch.

For a terrible moment, it has happened. Her worst nightmare has come true.

Then the other end of the board tips down and lands in the snow in front of her face.

"Whoa!" she hears her son muttering several times in a row with increasing volume. Then he bursts into an almost maniacal fit of laughter. "Are you seeing this, Mom?"

She looks up and lets out a startled gasp.

Sammy hangs in the air, floating freely midway between the rope bridge and the ground. He looks like something taken out of a NASA documentary. Or a science fiction movie.

She leans sideways and glances back over her shoulder.

Theodor is standing behind her, legs slightly apart, one arm at his side and the other outstretched with all the fingers of his hand halfway closed, as if holding an invisible handball.

Except that Yuki is aware that it's not a handball he's holding in the palm of his hand. It's her son.

"Get him down."

"I'm ... ugh ... trying," Theodor groans—and it's the truth. His tremoring hand and the beads of sweat on his forehead prove that much.

"It's okay, Mom. I'm not scared."

Perhaps not, but she is. So scared and so shaken that her legs almost collapse under her as she gets up.

Just when she reaches Sammy, he begins to descend. It looks bizarre. As if he's slowly sinking to the bottom of a waterless swimming pool.

She grabs him, wraps her arms around him, and pulls him close ... but Sammy doesn't return her embrace. He resists and tries to pull free.

"Let go of me, Mom! He's falling!"

A second later, there are two bumps as Theodor's knee—and then the entire left side of his body—hit the snow.

Yuki lets go, and Sammy rushes over to him.

"Theodor, are you okay?"

The old man is conscious, but for a moment, he looks as if he neither hears nor sees the boy.

"Your nose. You're bleeding."

After another moment of blankness, awareness dawns in Theodor's eyes, and he brings his hand up to his nose. When he studies it afterward, two of the fingers are red.

"Sammy, help me get him up," Yuki says, squatting down next to Theodor and grabbing his arm. "We need to get him inside."

"Seems all you do is run around, picking me up,

huh?" Theodor mutters with a cockiness that Yuki isn't convinced he actually feels.

For Sammy's sake, she does something similar; smiles at the comment, although she doesn't find it amusing at all.

Using his abilities clearly takes a toll on Theodor, and with the blank expression he had on his face after his fall, she has a feeling that things could have gone much worse.

That there might not have been a need to pick him up again if he had tried to keep Sammy floating for just a little while longer.

CHAPTER 37

After so many years of being married to a man like Dean, anxiety is by no means an unfamiliar emotion for Yuki. Countless times she has found herself in a situation where a misstep on her part may or may not have been big enough to trigger his anger. Sometimes she has even had to wait a very long time for the punishment to arrive. Because depending on his mood on the given day, Dean likes to pull out all the stops and put on a show.

So no, anxious anticipation is nothing new for Yuki. Therefore, the last few hours shouldn't have presented much of a challenge for her. Nevertheless, her palms have been sweaty and her head so full of worry that you'd think she was facing a difficult school exam.

And perhaps that isn't such a misleading analogy because she *is* afraid of failing. Afraid that the people from the crisis center will take one look at her and decide that she is nothing more than a hysterical lunatic. That she ought to go home and talk to her husband, rather than trying to steal beds from others who actually need help.

"Mom?" Sammy says, gently pulling on her jacket. "Theodor asked you a question."

"What? Oh, sorry. My mind was elsewhere."

"It's okay," Theodor says. He is the only one of them still inside the cabin, putting on his jacket. "I just asked if you have the keys."

Yuki checks her pocket and nods.

"Got 'em."

"Good. Then you guys can just go ahead and jump in the truck. I've got to turn off the generator and lock the cabin, and then I'll be right behind you."

"You don't want a hand?"

"To flick a switch and lock a door?" he asks with the dry, sarcastic tone that she, to her own surprise, has grown to like. "I think I'll manage."

"That's not what she meant," Sammy starts, but Yuki stops him by shaking her head.

"Theodor knows what I meant," she says, putting her arm around the boy's shoulders. Then she winks at Theodor and adds, "He's just got bad manners, that's all."

Even before they get in the car, Yuki feels a twinge of unease, and after taking a seat—her at the wheel,

Sammy in the back—it only gets worse. She just can't pinpoint what's triggering it.

Is it just that the truck makes her think of Dean? It sort of makes sense. Especially since this big, brawny Ford Raptor isn't just Dean's property. It's also a metaphorical mirror image of him; a ferocious, fine-tuned macho machine that doesn't stop for anything.

"Can you put some heat on?" Sammy asks from the back seat. "I can see my own breath."

To prove his point, he leans in between the seats and exhales so she can see it with her own eyes. And yes, in front of his lips, a small white cloud appears.

"I'll turn on the heat," she says, after which she puts the key in the ignition.

But when she turns it, nothing happens.

She tries again. Once ... twice ... still no response from the metal beast.

"That's weird," she murmurs, pulling out the key and looking at it as if expecting that staring it down will somehow solve the problem.

"Mom?"

"Just a sec. I'm thinking."

"But, Mom ..."

"Wait, Sammy! I'm trying to figure out why the car won't start."

"MOM!"

She jumps in her seat, almost dropping the key.

"What *is* it, Sammy?" she snaps, more than just a bit

annoyed, as she turns around in her seat and stares at him. However, her annoyance instantly disappears when she sees the fear in his eyes.

Without saying anything, he lifts a finger and points to something behind her. She follows the line from his finger, up toward the windshield ... and momentarily loses her ability to breathe.

Under the rearview mirror hangs an air freshener. A piece of perfumed cardboard in the shape of a pine tree. It's been hanging there forever, so there's nothing new about that. What is new, though, is the other thing that is now hanging next to the tree on the same string. A small, rectangular piece of cardboard, the jagged edges of which reveal that it has been torn free.

Oh yes, sometimes Dean really likes to pull out all the stops.

On the cardboard are eight blocky letters, together forming one word.

HOTHEADS.

"Sammy, we have to get back to the cabin. Now."

In her head, she's shouting, but the words come out of her mouth like a brittle, monotonous whisper. Nonetheless, the message—and the urgency—seem to have gotten through clearly to the boy, because he is already halfway out the door.

Riddled with panic and with the goal of getting to safety behind a locked door as her driving force, she follows Sammy. And due to her panic, it's only after they've come through the door that she realizes it ought to have been locked.

And by then it's too late.

"Speak of the devil," Dean says from the armchair, where he sits with one hand resting on the armrest and the other facing Theodor on the sofa.

The latter is the hand in which he holds the gun.

"My ... dear family has joined us," he says mockingly, after which he nods toward the couch. "Why don't you take a seat? We have some things we need to talk about."

PART VIII
HOTHEAD

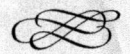

> "Heaven is a spot
> in the shade of a tree
> with a good book."
>
> Things Martha used to say

CHAPTER 38

"If you knew how much trouble you've caused me," Dean says, sending Yuki a smile devoid of warmth. "I had to break into my own workplace in the middle of the night to borrow one of the confiscated cars, just so I could get up here. Oh, and let's not forget about this ..."

He leans forward in the chair and uses his free hand to pull up one of his pant legs, exposing the blood-stained bandage wrapped around his lower leg.

"Seventeen stitches," he says, sucking air in between his clenched teeth. "I did it myself. Cost a hell of a lot of Jack Daniel's, but at least I didn't have to sit in the emergency room's waiting area for hours on end."

"How did you find us?"

She tries to harden herself, tries to sound as if his little, theatrical surprise hasn't made an impact. But she can hear the fear in her own voice—and so can he.

He leans forward and stares at her. She wants to look away, but there is still a remnant of his power over her left. Something that keeps her gaze fixed on his night-black pupils.

"I'll always find you, Yuki," he whispers. "Always."

The words float through the air, move through her ear canal, and then transform into hundreds of tiny spiders crawling around on the nerve strands in her body.

She has lost. Worse still, she will always lose. The monster in the armchair will always be there, waiting for her with his taunting, predatory smile. She'll never be able to—

"Now, there's one thing in all of this that I can't make sense of," Theodor says over on the couch.

His voice sounds muddy and strained ... which assures Yuki of one thing: Dean wasn't gentle when he brought Theodor to that couch.

"All right, Mr. Moody," Dean says after a moment of reflection. "I'll bite. What is it that you don't understand?"

"You're a cop, right?" Theodor says. "How on earth were you able to keep that job if you can't even get your own wife to respect you?"

What are you doing? Yuki thinks. *If you taunt him like that—*

The realization hits her once she sees Dean point both his gaze and his gun at Theodor on the couch—

and thus away from the doorway, where she's still standing with Sammy.

"I guess it must be the uniform," Theodor continues. "That's something people respect. Maybe you should have worn it at home once in a while, huh?"

Dean raises the gun higher, thus moving the aim from Theodor's chest to his face. But Yuki knows he won't pull the trigger now. And she's pretty sure that Theodor is also aware of it.

Five minutes ago, Dean might have chosen that approach ... but after an insult like that, a bullet in the head won't be nearly enough punishment. It's too easy. Too quick.

While Dean is distracted, she moves her hand behind Sammy's back and pulls gently on his jacket to get his attention. Once she has it, she nods toward the open door behind them and mimes her message.

Get ready to run.

Sammy's face turns stiff, and he shakes his head, but she was expecting that, so she immediately gives him another look. One that lets him know it's not a negotiation—and not before she's received a nod from him does she let her gaze shift back to Dean and Theodor. There she keeps it locked as she moves her hand up on Sammy's shoulder and slowly starts leading him toward the doorway.

"I see now that I was too nice to you earlier, Mr.

Moody," Dean says. "But don't worry, I'll fix that when I'm done talking to Yuki."

Hearing her name makes Yuki's heart skip a beat, and when she sees Dean start to turn his head back in their direction, she is again struck by the certainty of her defeat.

But once more, Theodor comes to their rescue.

"Women and old men," he scoffs. "You're a real tough guy, huh?"

Talking like that to Dean Rowley is the verbal equivalent of throwing a lit torch into a powder keg. And it's also, Yuki grasps right away, her cue.

So, when Dean jumps up from the armchair and lunges toward Theodor, she grabs Sammy's jacket again and pulls him with her.

CHAPTER 39

Waving a red scarf in front of an angry bull that's located less than two feet away is a gamble on Theodor's part. A *reckless* gamble, some might argue. Especially since he doesn't have full control over his powers yet.

But Theodor sees no other solution. His best chance has to be to get Yuki's husband on his feet, so it will hit harder when he falls.

During the first few seconds, everything goes according to plan: Dean jumps up from the armchair, throws himself toward him, and Theodor uses all his energy to get the armchair to follow him.

The full weight of the floating chair hits Dean in the back just as he is about to close his large hand around Theodor's neck, causing him to lose his balance. He tumbles sideways and trips over the armrest of the couch with the grace of a dying fish, cursing and growling all the while.

Nevertheless, the joy of victory is short-lived for Theodor, because the big policeman is up again in no time, and it doesn't look as if the armchair has hurt him. It has confused and pissed him off even more, perhaps, but not hurt him.

Anticipating the inevitable consequence, Theodor curls up on the couch, holding his arms up in front of him. But Dean remains in place, and his gaze isn't on Theodor. Instead, it wanders back and forth on the living room floor near the couch and the overturned armchair. As if he's looking for something.

The gun. He's dropped the gun.

Now Dean crouches, looks farther ahead—under the big cabinet by the south wall of the cabin—and then the hint of a smile appears in the corners of his mouth.

He marches over to the cabinet, gets down on his knees, grabs the lower edge with one hand, and tries to lift it up so he can pick up the gun with the other hand.

The cabinet doesn't budge an inch ... but small droplets of blood start to creep out of Theodor's nostrils.

"What the fuck?" Dean grumbles, now grabbing the cabinet with both hands. He pulls and tugs until the skin around his eyes is bluish-purple, but the result remains the same. The cabinet stays where it is.

How long Theodor can hold his end of the invisible rope, however, he isn't sure, because the edges of his field of vision are starting to fill with dark gray clouds.

A sound from outside the cabin—a flock of birds shrieking—becomes his rescue as it makes Dean look toward the doorway where Yuki and Sammy were standing but moments ago.

He lets go of the cabinet, focuses his gaze on Theodor, and lets out a deep, guttural snarl. He both looks and sounds like a wild animal now; eyes bloodshot, nostrils pulsating, and teeth bared.

Theodor raises his hand trying to use the last of his strength to pull the cabinet down on his opponent's back, but Dean is too fast. He traverses the distance to the couch in two large steps, after which his arm shoots forward and grabs Theodor's wrist. Subsequently, he twists Theodor around and, with a policeman's perfected technique, presses his hand up between the shoulder blades on his back.

"We aren't done with each other, Mr. Moody," he whispers into Theodor's ear. "But right now, I need to have a serious talk with my family."

As he speaks, he gives Theodor's hand an extra push upwards, making it feel as if his whole arm is about to break off at the shoulder. Then he empties Theodor's lungs by hammering a fist into his side.

"Stay here, Mr. Moody. I'll be back before you know it."

Those words are the last thing Theodor hears before

Dean lets go and he rolls limply over the edge of the couch.

He lands on the cabin's hard, wooden floor—which right now feels as unsteady and swaying as a ship's deck during a storm.

It's also from there that he watches helplessly as Dean's foggy silhouette disappears out the door.

CHAPTER 40

Leaving Theodor alone in the cabin with a monster that she has brought into his life weighs heavily on Yuki. Especially because she can hear the noises from inside the house as she runs across the driveway with Sammy; a loud crack, as if a piece of furniture is being knocked over, followed by Dean's voice spewing out a swarm of profanities.

But as much as she hates leaving Theodor behind, she has no choice. Her number one priority must be to get Sammy away from Dean.

But how? Even if we make it all the way to the forest, there is snow everywhere. We might as well run around with a giant cardboard sign; WE'RE HERE, DEAN!

She scans her surroundings, trying to keep a clear head while doing so, but it's hard because the panic is threatening to take the wheel and steer her body.

The truck? Useless. It won't start. The woodshed? Too predictable. Look for Dean's new car? Forget it. You don't have the key to it. Come on, Yuki, think! Think!

Her gaze slides down to the lake, around the shore, over to the trees, and from there slightly upward.

It's far from perfect, but it's their best bet, and the hourglass is running out.

"We'll have to split up, sweetie," she says, crouching down in front of Sammy.

"But I—"

"No, Sammy. No *buts*. There's no time. You'll just have to trust me, okay?"

The boy frowns but nods anyway.

"We'll run that way," she continues, pointing down at the trees on the lakeshore. "And when we get to the fort, I want you to climb up there and hide. And this is important, Sammy: From now on, I'll take point and you follow in my footsteps. *Only* in my footsteps. Got it?"

"So he can't see mine?"

"Exactly. And as soon as you get up there, you pull the ladder up, okay? As *soon* as you're up there. And you don't let it down unless I'm the one telling you to. Got it?"

Sammy nods, and she gives him a kiss on the forehead.

"Good. Then let's go!"

Following her plan, they run—Yuki leading the way and Sammy jumping from one of her footprints to another—until they've reached the rope ladder leading up to the fort.

"And what won't you forget?" Yuki asks as Sammy begins to climb it.

"Just you. Otherwise, the ladder stays up."

"Exactly. And ... I love you, sweetie."

"I love you too, Mom."

Yuki waits until he starts pulling the ladder up, after which she hurries on, running along the shore of the lake. However, she doesn't get very far before a flock of birds in a bush is startled by her presence. They take off simultaneously, enveloping her in a jumble of flapping wings and frantic shrieks.

For a moment, the shock makes her freeze, but she shakes it off and speeds up again.

It's not that she's planning to run away from Dean. She's not *that* naive. But the more distance she can put between him and herself, the more time she'll have to figure out how to stop him.

Stop him? What are you going to do? Kill him?

The thought makes her wince—and the answer even more.

Do I have any other option?

Either way, she'll need a weapon if she's going to stand a chance. Therefore, she steers away from the lake and heads toward the nearest trees.

A thick branch will do. A rock with the right weight and size will do better.

That's the last thing she has time to think before the hourglass' final grain of sand falls and Dean's deep, hateful voice reverberates through the valley.

"YUKI! SAMMY! WHERE ARE YOU?"

A pause. Then the voice returns, spiced with a touch of mockery. As if he wants to emphasize how naive it is to think that they can escape him.

"SO, YOU WANT TO PLAY, HUH? FINE, THEN LET'S PLAY! THREE ... TWO ... ONE! I'M COMING!"

Yuki picks up the pace, forcing her body to push aside the fear and run while her gaze desperately searches for a hiding place.

The possibilities are sparse, but she does spot a cave-like hole under the gnarled roots of an old, windthrown pine tree on top of a small hill where the forest area begins.

The distance is a bit longer than she would have liked, but on the other hand, the large cluster of the tree's roots protruding from the ceiling of the hole has given her an idea.

When she has reached the hole under the tree, she glances back. Neither the cabin nor Dean can be seen from here ... which means he can't see her either.

She unzips her red parka and pulls it off. Next, she edges past the front cluster of roots hanging from the ceiling of the hole and hangs the coat on a few of the roots in the back.

When she feels certain that the coat is visible from

the outside—but not too obvious—she hurries back and uses the front roots to climb up to the tree itself, on the hill above the cave.

The roots are covered with a thin layer of snow, some of which falls off as she climbs up. There is nothing she can do about that. She'll just have to hope that Dean will think it's because she's bumped against the roots while crawling into the cave to hide.

"YUKI! SAMMY! WHERE ARE YOU?"

The sound of his voice is loud. But it's not just that. She can also hear the snow crunching under his boots. He's close now. Too close. The only positive thing is that he must have walked right past the fort without spotting Sammy.

She slides to her knees, crawls into hiding on the other side of the tree, and starts digging in the snow with her bare hands.

The cold makes it feel like she's submerged both hands in a tub of hydrochloric acid. Still, what hurts the most is the fact that she doesn't find anything useful. Frozen dirt, frozen twigs, frozen pinecones, frozen—

Her train of thought derails as her fingertips encounter a hard, jagged surface. She locates the edges, grabs them, and starts wiggling from side to side.

The moment the rock breaks loose, she hears a faint crunch.

It's coming from below. As in *just below* her.

Slowly—infinitely slowly—she brings the rock with

her and crawls back to the other side of the tree, seating herself just above the exit of the cave.

She waits—for one particular sound that she knows will come. Yet, she is so startled when she hears it that she is on the verge of tipping over the edge.

A *'riisch'*—as in the sound of a jacket being ripped free of what it's hanging on—followed by a frustrated snarl.

Yuki lifts the rock up above her head, ready to bring it down on her husband when he comes rushing out of the cave in a second. Ready to stop him once and for—

Yuki gets no further. Because Dean doesn't come rushing out of the cave. Instead, he grabs the roots and —quite literally—pulls the ground out from under her.

CHAPTER 41

It feels like Yuki's torso is in flames. As if the skin on her back and stomach is melting.

In fact, the opposite is true. Her upper body is being cooled down because her blouse has slipped open and thus is filled with chunks of snow and ice as Dean drags her mercilessly across the ground.

He's got her by the ankle. At first, she fought back and tried to break free, but she quickly ran out of energy, so now she's just trying to stay conscious. And to avoid getting her mouth and nose filled with snow when a bump in the terrain occasionally flips her around so she ends up face down.

The constant blows to her back—rocks, branches, and chunks of ice—also make it virtually impossible for her to breathe properly, so when Dean finally stops and lets her go, she can do nothing but lie on the ground, gasping for air.

"Now, listen carefully, you little bitch," he hisses, leaning over her. "Because I'm only going to ask you once. Where is Sammy?"

She wants to tell him that he can go to hell, but all that comes out of her mouth is a half-choked cough and a pink mixture of saliva and blood.

An intense pain shoots down her neck and spine as Dean grabs her again, this time by the hair, and pulls her onward, grunting and muttering to himself.

"Knock me over the head with a rock. A fucking *rock*! Dumbass bitch. Should have strangled you a long time ago."

A new, paralyzing shock hits her when the snow underneath her suddenly disappears and is replaced with a smooth—but still bitterly cold—surface.

Ice. Dean has dragged her out onto the lake.

Panic grips her, makes her writhe from side to side, makes her punch and kick and scream like a madwoman. It's done blindly because he's still holding her by the hair, but at some point, she manages to grab his forearm—and dig her nails so deep into his skin that it feels like they're going to break off.

She doesn't care. She presses harder, and then she pulls until she can feel his skin give way and curl off in shreds under her nails. Until she can feel the heat of his blood spreading like a glove over her hand.

"AAARGH! I'M GONNA KILL YOU, YOU FUCKING WHORE!" he roars—and before Yuki can react, he has pulled his wounded hand out of her grip. But he doesn't waste time tending to it. Instead, he moves it farther down and grabs her blouse. Then he drags her around violently in a semicircle and lets go.

Unable to do anything to prevent it, Yuki slides across the frozen surface of the lake on her naked, aching back—out to where the ice is thinner.

Now she lies there, once again gasping for air, staring up at the gray sky of the afternoon, listening to the sound of Dean's steps reverberating in the ice beneath her.

In a moment, it will be over. She knows this, in her heart and in her soul. Because he's not going to let her walk away from this. He is going to—

A new sound blends with Dean's footsteps, and it hits her like a shot of adrenaline in the heart.

It's also footsteps, but ... the sound is lighter and the intervals are shorter.

"NO, SAMMY! NO!" she screams, but it's too late. When she turns her head and looks, the boy has come all the way up behind Dean.

"LEAVE HER ALONE!" he roars as he starts pounding away at his father's back. "LEAVE MOM ALONE!"

"Your mother is sick, Sammy," Dean says. "We can't help her."

"NO, SHE'S NOT!" Sammy screams, still throwing punches to no avail. "*YOU'RE* THE ONE WHO IS SICK!"

Dean glances over at Yuki and sighs deeply as if to say: *You see what you've done?* Afterward, he turns back to Sammy and puts his huge hand—the bloody one that Yuki scratched, mind you—on the boy's cheek. For a brief moment, it could be mistaken for a caress, but then the hand continues to the back of Sammy's head and grabs his hair.

Dean's message to the boy is subdued, little more than a whisper, yet every heartbreaking word somehow travels all the way to Yuki's ears.

"How I could actually believe that such a whiny loser could be my son, I don't know. I should have figured it out a long time ago ... with the way your whore of a mother bats her sheep eyes at every fucking man she sees."

Desperate to come to her son's aid, Yuki starts dragging herself across the ice. However, she doesn't get very far before Sammy comes to her instead. Sliding helplessly across the ice, just as she did a few moments ago.

She grabs his jacket, pulls him over to her, and hugs him. He trembles and sobs—and so does she.

"You'll never get away with this," she says. "Police brothers or not, they won't let this slide. You've gone too far this time."

Dean gives her a cryptic smile and slowly shakes his head.

"Do I look worried?" he says. "Look around. You've almost made it too easy."

He spreads his arms and spins around himself to direct her attention to their surroundings.

"I won't have to pull any strings or ask for any favors at all. Because it was an accident, wasn't it?"

He moves closer but with slow, theatrical steps. It's almost as if he's trying to drag out the moment.

"A terrible, terrible tragedy," he continues. "Mother and child, drowned in a forest lake because their car slid off the icy road and went down a hillside."

He points up to the landscape behind the eastern end of the lake, which—quite rightly—has a long slope that ends up by the road.

"Right into the lake," he finishes as he stops in front of them and crouches. "Simple, right? You've even got the car ready for me and everything."

He stretches his hand out toward her. She pushes it away, but he keeps going, over and over again, like a hyena snapping at its prey until it's too tired to fight back. And when her arms finally give up, he grabs her hair once more. Then he pulls upward and leans in close, his face right next to hers.

"All I need now is something hard to punch a hole in the ice," he whispers with his lips pressed against her cheek.

She opens her mouth with the intention of begging him one last time to show mercy and let Sammy go, but before she can say anything, her head is forced down in a quick jerk.

One, two, three times he smashes it into the blank surface of the lake. The ice holds, but her face feels on the verge of cracking, and streams of blood run down her forehead and into her eyes, making the snowy landscape around her look like she's watching it through a pale red lens.

So does the silhouette she spots on the ice some distance behind Dean. It's reddish, almost purple. Maybe it's just a figment of her imagination, but it seems to ... come closer?

Theodor? He's not—

The thought is brutally ripped apart as Dean once again hammers her face into the ice.

The world is no longer pale red. It's dark brown, and it's flickering unsteadily like an old TV. It is, she understands somewhere in her consciousness, moving away from her.

But Theodor's blurry figure is still behind Dean—and now he's raising his arm as if he's pointing to something over to the right.

Except that he isn't pointing, because all his fingers are outstretched, and ...

The realization hits—and awakens—her, like a bucket of cold water in her face would have done. She squints, forcing her eyes to focus, and follows the invisible line from his hand over to the tree by the shore.

The tall, half-rotten birch tree, which is now slowly starting to lean further and further out over the lake.

From the soil under the tree comes a series of small pops. In all probability, it's the sound of roots breaking.

Dean has also noticed it. At least that's what she assumes since he has loosened his grip on her hair.

This is your chance, she thinks, and immediately, almost as an extension of that thought, Theodor's voice roars through the air.

"YUKI! GET SAMMY AWAY FROM THERE!"

In one last effort, she mobilizes all her remaining willpower and uses it to pull free of Dean's hands. Next, she spins herself around in one fluent motion, using the smooth surface of the ice, so her feet end up pointing toward Dean's face.

And then she kicks.

CHAPTER 42

As he stands out there on the frozen lake, watching Yuki and Sammy running away from Dean, Theodor realizes he's made a mistake. He's put in too much effort from the start, pulled too hard, and if he doesn't do something, the tree will fall into the lake before they've reached safety. Its roots are already snapping with both the speed and the sound of a burning hot pot of popcorn.

He tries to slow the tree's fall, but gravity is a phenomenal opponent. It presses him until his hands tremble uncontrollably, and his mouth fills with the rusty taste from the blood seeping out of his nose and down over his lips. And even then, it doesn't hold back.

"HURRY UP!" he yells at Yuki and Sammy, who still need to run at least fifteen or twenty yards more across the ice to be out of the danger zone. "I ... CAN'T ... HOLD IT!"

To make matters worse, he now sees that Dean has shifted his focus away from his own bloody nose and is back on his feet. Yuki and Sammy have a head start, but he is physically superior to them in every respect, and he is already catching up with them.

Knowing that it will take everything he has left in him, Theodor makes his decision. He releases his invisible grip on the tree and points his hands at Sammy and Yuki instead.

And then he pulls.

The effort exhausts him, forces him to his knees, and blurs his vision.

But he makes it. Just as the tree breaks through the frozen surface of the lake, creating a giant cobweb of large cracks, he sees Yuki and Sammy sliding by on either side of him.

The two people he has come to love so much are safe.

This is the thought he clings to as fresh cracks appear around him, tearing away more and more chunks of ice. Opening the gateway down to the water. To the icy, deadly darkness of the forest lake.

It has already taken Dean. It has soaked him from head to toe and now pulls him relentlessly downward, ripping the surrounding ice slabs out of his hands every time he reaches for them.

In a few seconds, the water will take Theodor as well, and he'll be unable to fight back.

When the moment occurs and the ice starts to move underneath his knees, he instinctively closes his eyes and prepares to be grabbed and pulled down into the deep.

Something does grab him, but it's not the water. It's human hands, closing their fingers around his arms and pulling him backward.

He opens his eyes. The first thing he sees is his own legs being hauled backward in a race against all the new cracks constantly appearing in the ice a few feet ahead. The second thing he sees is Yuki and Sammy on either side of him, both struggling to pull him. They look like something taken straight out of a nightmare. Her face is swollen and bruised, and he has a red smudge on his cheek that looks like a handprint.

"Just a little longer, sweetie," Yuki groans. She sounds like she's on the verge of passing out from exhaustion. "We're ... almost there."

"I know, Mom. I know."

Theodor tries to help by kicking with his feet, but his boots just slide around aimlessly, and it makes no difference.

Fifty feet from the shore, they have reached safety, and the ice has stopped cracking. Still, Yuki and Sammy keep pulling until they're on the shore ... after which they both let go and tumble to the ground.

For a long time, all three of them lie there on their backs with their eyes fixed on the gray clouds in the sky, listening to each other's breathing as it gradually calms.

"It's over," Yuki suddenly says.

"And what about Dad?" Sammy asks. "Is he ...?"

"It's over," Theodor repeats.

And Sammy doesn't ask again.

CHAPTER 43

"911. What's your emergency?"

"I ... oh God, there's been a terrible accident. It's my husband. Our truck slid off the road and he ... oh God."

"Take a deep breath, ma'am. Can you tell me what happened to your husband?"

"The road was slippery, and our truck went down a slope and my husband couldn't get it to slow down, so it ..."

"Yes?"

"So, it kept going, out on the lake. On the ice. It went through and ... it sank."

"Your vehicle sank into the lake?"

"Y-yes. ... oh God, and my husband couldn't get out, he ... he's dead. He drowned."

"I'll send out a unit right away, ma'am. Are you at the scene of the accident right now?"

"Yes, I ... yes, I am. I'm with my son. He was in the truck too."

"Okay. Can you give me an address?"

"We're in Maiden Lake."

"Do you have a street name?"

"Um, no, it's ... it's the big one, the main road. I don't know what it's called. We're down by the lake."

"Okay. They'll find it on the GPS. And you said that you and your son are okay, correct?"

"What? Yeah, we're okay. Wet and cold, but okay."

"I see. I'll send an extra ambulance just in case."

"Okay ... and thank you."

"No problem. You're doing fine, ma'am. May I ask for your name?"

"Yes, sure. My name is Yuki Rowley, and my son's name is Samuel, but um ... we just call him Sammy."

"Okay. Listen, Yuki. The ambulance will be with you in ten to fifteen minutes. Until then, I'd like to ask you to do something for me. You need to make sure to keep Sammy—and yourself—as warm as possible. Do you think you can do that?"

"Y-yeah, um, of course. I will."

"Perfect. Then I'll hang up now. Help is on the way, okay?"

"Okay. Bye ... and um, thank you so much."

"You're welcome. Bye."

TWO YEARS LATER

EPILOGUE

"Are you going to answer that?"

"What?"

"Are you going to answer it?" Kimberly repeats from the kitchen. "Your phone! It's ringing!"

"Oh, sorry. I'm in the bathroom. I didn't hear it. Would you mind getting it? I'm ... drying my hair."

That's a lie. Kevin's hair is dry, and what he is actually doing—tying his tie—he could easily take a break from. But he doesn't feel like talking on the phone right now. Especially not if he's right in his guess about who's on the other end.

"Hi, Mom," sounds from the kitchen.

Ding-ding-ding! Your mother-in-law is on the phone. The first prize goes to Kevin Moody!

"Kevin can't talk right now, Mom. Drying his hair.

We're going to that meeting today. With the lawyer. Yeah, about Theodor."

His double Windsor knot is done. Yet, Kevin remains in front of the bathroom mirror with the end of the tie in his hand for a good while. If he goes out there straight away, he risks getting handed the phone, but if mother and daughter get a moment to warm up their jaws, he should be home free.

"Don't worry about that, Mom," Kimberly continues. "No one expected you to interrupt your holiday and leave Rome early when it wasn't even close family. I already wrote that to you."

A pause.

"Yeah, it was a nice funeral. Surprisingly many, actually. Especially considering … yeah, well, you know what Theodor could be like sometimes. Yeah, I think so too. Everybody liked her."

Gossip. The coast must be clearing, Kevin concludes as he puts on his suit jacket and tiptoes out into the hallway. From there he can look into the kitchen.

The index finger of Kimberly's free hand moves in circles, making small curls in her bangs. Yep, the coast is clear.

"Not at all," Kimberly says. "As I wrote in the text, it was very peaceful. In his own bed, quietly. The cleaning lady did. Yeah, she had a key, so when she came in to work the next morning … well, he was just lying there."

When Kevin enters the kitchen and edges past her, Kimberly looks up at him and smiles. He responds by tapping his wristwatch.

I'm trying, she mimes, raising her hand and making a gesture that looks like a crocodile snapping.

"Kevin says hello, Mom. No, no. He's doing okay. He's just glad he didn't suffer. Listen, Mom, I'm going to have to go now. Otherwise, we'll be late for that meeting. Uh-huh, I will. You say hi to Dad from me, and ... yeah, we sure will. Bye, Mom."

She takes the phone from her ear and lets out a long, exhausted sigh. Then she hands the phone to Kevin.

"Next time, *you* answer it."

"But it was *your* mother."

"A *thank you, babe* would have sufficed. Are you ready?"

Kevin leans in and gives her a kiss on the cheek while snatching the cell phone from her hand.

"Thanks, babe."

"You're terrible."

"So what? I'm still a rock star. I got my rock moves."

Twenty minutes later, Kevin still has Pink's monster hit stuck in his brain as he pushes his Audi up to ninety miles per hour and pulls out into the fast lane.

"By the way, I got a response from Chaney this morning," Kimberly says in the passenger seat.

"Who?"

"Owen Chaney. The architect. The genius who designed the gazebo in Tori and Callum's garden."

"Oh yeah, Chaney! So, what did he say?"

Kimberly responds by lifting up her sunglasses so he can see her winking.

"He said yes?"

"He said yes!" Kimberly repeats. "He's got a full calendar, but when I told him about the place and the surroundings, he couldn't resist. So now we just need to sort out the paperwork, and as soon as it's officially ours, he can start sketching."

Kevin juts out his lower lip and nods his head back and forth in recognition. Then he gives the top edge of the steering wheel a slap with a flat hand.

"It's going to be so fucking great, Kim! A real house instead of a rundown old cabin. And then away with all the trees that block the view of the lake. It's going to be a fucking Hollywood home!"

"It should have been done a long time ago," Kimberly says. "I don't get why he was so stubborn about it. He didn't even have to set foot up there. He could have just hired someone to fix it and then rented it out. He could have made a fortune."

"To piss us off."

"You really think it was just that?"

"Oh, come on. What else? He knew we wanted the cabin, and yet he left it empty for years."

Kimberly squints for a moment and then shakes her head.

"Nah, I don't know. After all, a lot of the time it was more bark than bite with him. Maybe it was just the thought of getting rid of the place that was too painful for him. With all the memories, you know."

Kevin turns his face and stares at her as if she has just said that a YouTube video has convinced her that the Earth is actually flat.

"Oh, give me a break, Kimberly. We're talking about my dad. My old, petty, racist, half-demented—God bless his soul—faultfinder of a father. Not exactly Mr. Bleeding Heart. I know he gave me a hard time for not visiting Mom enough when she was sick ... but that's what it was about. Giving me a hard time. It wasn't him feeling bad for Mom. It was him being on my back. As always."

Kimberly shrugs, which isn't quite the support Kevin had hoped for, but he doesn't want to waste time getting annoyed about that. Not today. Because today is going to be a good day.

"It doesn't even matter anyway," he says. "After the meeting today, the cabin will be ours, and then the old fart can twist in his grave as much as he wants."

"You do know he's going to haunt your sorry ass if he gets the chance, right?"

Kevin lets out a sputtering laugh but then catches himself in it and stifles it again.

In the passenger seat, Kimberly's face also takes on a more solemn expression. Clearly, she too has reached the conclusion that the last comment crossed the line. After all, it's his father they're talking about, and it's been less than a week since they put him in the ground.

SHARP & BELL—ATTORNEYS AT LAW is located on Poplar Street in Gleamsdale, sandwiched between a bakery and a watchmaker. Common to these three enterprises is the number of parking spaces they have available to their customers, which is none whatsoever. Therefore, Kevin and Kimberly are forced to park the Audi three blocks away—next to a construction site surrounded by a cloud of concrete dust—and walk the rest of the way on foot.

Upon entering the law firm, they are greeted by a young woman behind a counter who only reluctantly puts away her cell phone as they approach her.

"Hi, we have a meeting with Warren Sharp about—"

"The Moody will, right?" the secretary interrupts, nodding. "Up the stairs, first office on the right. You can head on up. The others are already here."

"The others?"

"Uh-huh, yeah," the young woman says, raising one eyebrow. Then she nods in the direction of the stairs. "They're waiting for you."

Kevin and Kimberly exchange a confused look and then turn back to the secretary, but her focus is no longer on them. It's back on her phone.

Baffled—and pretty annoyed—they back away from the counter and walk up the stairs to the office on the first floor.

WARREN F. SHARP, SENIOR PARTNER is written on an oval bronze sign on the door.

Kevin knocks gently, listens for a moment, and then knocks again.

"Come on in!" says a man's voice.

Kevin and Kimberly open the door, step over the threshold—and then both stiffen so synchronously that you'd think they'd practiced it from home.

"Mr. and Mrs. Moody," the lawyer says, extending his hand. "Welcome."

Neither Kevin nor Kimberly takes his hand. In fact, none of them even pay any attention to the gray-haired man in the striped suit in front of them, although he presumably must be WARREN F. SHARP, SENIOR PARTNER.

"W-what are they doing here?"

The lawyer glances down at his own hand, still hanging in the air. Then he pulls it back and follows Kevin's gaze to the table in the center of the office.

"This is Yuki Wanchai and her son, Samuel Wanchai," the lawyer says as if that explains anything.

"*We know* who they are," Kimberly says. "That's not what Kevin asked. What are they doing here?"

The lawyer adjusts his glasses, smiling uncertainly.

Then he clears his throat and makes a sweeping motion toward the table with his hand.

"If you would take a seat, I'm sure it'll all make sense in a moment."

Hesitantly, Kevin and Kimberly walk over to the table, pull out a couple of chairs, and sit down. Both the cleaning lady and her son greet them with a friendly nod—which Kevin pretends he doesn't see.

"Excellent," the lawyer says, after which he pulls out a brown cardboard folder from his filing cabinet and brings it to the table. "As you know, we are gathered here to review Theodor Moody's will, in which everyone present is mentioned."

He looks around, receiving nods from all of them.

"The will was put in my care when Theodor made the last change, just over a year ago, which is also when he asked me to arrange this meeting. The wording is very straightforward, so it should be pretty clear, but if any questions do arise, please let me know."

Is he kidding? Kevin thinks. *If any questions arise? Oh, I have a fucking question: What the hell are those two doing here?*

"Well, we'd better get to it," the lawyer continues. "Theodor's primary assets included the house on Rue Lane, which he owned, $119,302 in deposits in various bank accounts, as well as stocks and bonds, and finally the vacation home in Maiden Lake and the associated piece of land."

Kevin lays his hand on Kimberly's forearm and gives it a light squeeze. She smiles.

"In addition, some specified possessions are to be distributed separately ... but that's all explained in the statement."

"The statement?"

"Yes, um, Theodor made a statement, a letter, if you will, which he insisted that I read aloud on this day."

Kevin's eyes narrow, becoming two thin lines, but he says nothing.

"To my son, Kevin, my daughter-in-law, Kimberly, my cleaning lady, Yuki, and my good friend, Sammy," the lawyer reads aloud. "Apparently, I've kicked the bucket. It's regrettable, not least for me, but there's no changing it, so please don't make a big deal out of it."

The lawyer skims a little further in the text without articulating the words. Then he clears his throat.

"The next piece is a pure formality—the signatory, Theodor Moody, healthy in both body and mind, declares that ... that sort of thing. I'll skip straight to the distribution, okay?"

"Yeah, please do."

"I leave my fortune, meaning all the funds in my bank accounts and my shares to my son, Kevin, who is very fond of money."

The lawyer looks up, Kevin nods and shrugs.

"Likewise, I leave my house on Rue Lane to Kevin, including all inventory and all belongings of value ...

with two exceptions. One of these is Martha's jewelry, which is to go to my daughter-in-law, Kimberly. Martha would have wanted that."

Kevin and Kimberly look at each other with the same look of surprise.

"The other exception is my tools out in the garage. It is my wish that these will go to Sammy Wanchai. He'll need them if his bike breaks again."

Out of the corner of his eye, Kevin sees the cleaning lady stroke her hand over her son's back and send him a sad smile. It's a bit nauseating ... but what the hell. Now, at least, he knows why they were invited to the meeting. So that the little punk could inherit a bunch of old, rusty screwdrivers and pliers—and whatever else the old geezer had lying out there in the garage, collecting dust. Not exactly a big loss for Kevin. Saves him a trip to the junkyard.

"And the last asset?" Kimberly asks.

"Yes, um ... it comes as a continuation of the part about the bike," the lawyer says, swallowing with a clear click before he starts reading aloud again. "Furthermore, Sammy will need some proper tools to help his mother with maintenance and repairs as it is my decision that the cabin in Maiden Lake and the associated land will go to Yuki Wanchai."

For the first couple of seconds, Kevin's brain simply can't compute the information, but when he looks over to the other side of the table and sees the cleaning lady, it hits him like a baseball bat in the stomach. She's sitting with both hands covering her mouth and tearful eyes.

"This can't be right," he says. "There must have been some mistake."

"Are we sure he even knew what he was signing?" Kimberly adds. "His mind wasn't always right, and he had trouble remembering things."

"I assure you that Mr. Moody was of sound mind when he made this statement," the lawyer says.

Kevin feels an urge—a very strong urge—to jump up from his chair and rip the paper out of the lawyer's hands, but he calms down and nods instead.

"Now, where were we?" the lawyer mumbles, after which he fumbles a bit with the paper before starting to read out loud again. "I know it will come as a surprise to Kevin and Kimberly, but I'm also convinced that they'll eventually come to understand my decision. Because it *is* the right one. I know it is, Kevin, because I've listened to your mother. Martha was my moral compass when she was alive, and she still is. She would have wanted the cabin to go to Yuki and Sammy so it could continue to be a sanctuary for them as it has been for the past few years. Just like it always was for Martha. A church serves best those ..."

"... who look up when standing in it," Kevin finishes,

and when the lawyer gives him an inquisitive look, he bites his lower lip and turns his gaze downward. "It was, um ... something my mother used to say."

For a long time, nobody comments on that. All of them just stare silently at each other—and at Kevin in particular.

In a way, this includes himself, because, at this moment, his mother's profound words have made him look inward, harder than ever before.

Something brushes his arm. It's Kimberly. She stares at him with her bright blue eyes. Then she closes and opens her eyelids slowly as if to tell him to go ahead. That it's okay.

Kevin takes a breath and nods. Then he puts his hand in his pocket and pulls out a bundle of keys. From it, he removes a single key, which he slides across the table so it ends up in front of Yuki.

She picks it up, studies it for a moment while it's lying in the palm of her hand, and then closes her fingers around it. Next, she leans over to her son, smiles at him, and receives a smile back.

However, Kevin notices that it's only their lips that carry those smiles. Above them, their eyes are full of a deep sadness, the authenticity of which he couldn't deny, even if he wanted to.

The rest of the meeting takes place in almost complete silence. The lawyer is practically doing all the talking, and that's only because he has to ask for their signatures on a handful of legal documents.

When it's over, Kevin and Kimberly are the first to leave the office. That, too, is done in silence. They get up, nod their polite goodbyes to the lawyer—and as soon as that's done, they hurry out the door and down the stairs.

As they leave the building and step out into the street, the glass door only just has time to close behind them before it's pushed open again, and a bright voice says:

"Excuse me, Mr. Moody?"

Kevin turns around and sees the cleaning lady's son.

"Hi, kid. What's up?"

For a moment, the boy seems oddly nervous. As if he's been caught in a prank and is afraid he's going to get yelled at.

"I, um ... I've got something that I thought you might want."

A cabin in Maiden Lake, perhaps? Kevin thinks, but he says nothing.

"It's this," the boy says, putting his hand in his jacket pocket. When it reappears, an old carving knife is resting in his palm. "When, um ... when we were up in the cabin, Theodor sometimes let me borrow this to carve wood if I promised to take good care of it. And well, since it's yours, I thought you might want it back."

Kevin takes the knife, turns it around, and reads his

own name engraved in the handle with a child's large, uneven letters. It feels heavy. Way too heavy for its size.

"He really kept this all those years?"

The boy shrugs but remains silent. Behind him, his mother appears in the entrance door of the law office. She looks down at the knife in Kevin's hand, then at the boy.

"We'd better get home, sweetie."

The boy starts to turn around, but Kevin—driven by a sudden impulse—stops him by placing a hand on his shoulder.

"It's Sammy, right?"

The boy nods, and Kevin hands him the knife.

"I think you should keep it, Sammy. As a thank you for taking such good care of my father."

The boy looks up at his mother, who hesitates for a long moment before giving him her blessing with a nod.

As the boy accepts the gift, Kevin meets the cleaning lady's gaze.

"I have to admit, he wasn't lying, my dad."

"About what?"

"What he said when the two of us first met," Kevin elaborates. "You really do take good care of your elders where you come from."

For a moment, Yuki gawks at him as if he was speaking to her in a foreign language. Then her lips curl up in a warm smile.

"That's true," she says. "Although I'm not sure that

Theodor ever found out where I'm actually from. Had someone asked him, he probably would have told them I was Chinese."

"Theodor Moody in a nutshell," Kevin says.

"In a nutshell," Yuki repeats.

And then they go their separate ways.

THANKS TO ...

Sarah Jacobsen, my eternal first reader and co-conspirator in this life. My Martha.

Kaare and Karina Bertelsen Dantoft, my usual beta readers. Invaluable help.

All the grumpy old men I've encountered at post offices, park benches, train stations, and pharmacy lines. Without you, there would've been no Theodor Moody.

Last—but never least—I owe a huge thank you to you, dear reader. Our time is precious, and I thank you from the bottom of my heart for yours.

—Per Jacobsen

Printed in Dunstable, United Kingdom